Winged Warfare

Lt. Col. William A. Bishop, V.C., D.S.O., M.C.
ROYAL FLYING CORPS

Winged Warfare

edited by Stanley M. Ulanoff Lt. Col., USAR

Pan Books London and Sydney

Published in Great Britain 1975 by Bailey Brothers and Swinfen Ltd
This edition published 1978 by Pan Books Ltd,
Cavaye Place, London SW10 9PG
© Stanley M. Ulanoff 1967
ISBN 0 330 25443 X
Printed and bound in Great Britain by
Richard Clay (The Chaucer Press) Ltd, Bungay, Suffolk

ACKNOWLEDGMENTS

None have been more co-operative in this undertaking – publishing anew Air Marshal William A. Bishop's dramatic story of World War I air combat, than the Canadian Government through its Department of National Defence and Canadian Forces Headquarters. They have been most helpful in furnishing me with photos, historical information and records.

As always Lieutenant Colonel Bob Webb and Mrs. Anna C. Urband of the Magazine and Book Branch of the Office of the U. S. Assistant Secretary of Defence for Public Affairs have given their customary wholhearted support and assistance.

I must also acknowledge the contribution of Revell, Inc. and Joe Phelan who furnished their fine three-view drawings of First World War fighter planes to me.

In closing I proffer my thanks to Mrs. Wm. A. Bishop and her son W. Arthur Bishop for making available the valuable original manuscript of *Winged Warfare*, which has long been out of print, and consenting to its publication in our new series, Air Combat Classics.

And 'last but not least' go my appreciation to my assistant Alan Matcovsky for typing the difficult charts and tables in the Appendix, the Introduction, and this Acknowledgment; and to the wonderful Xerox 2400 that permitted me to make first-rate copies of the entire manuscript without damage to it.

STANLEY M. ULANOFF
Editor

CONTENTS

INTRODUCTION BY STANLEY M. ULANOFF   13

WINGED WARFARE   19

APPENDIX:

Chronology of World War I   225

   Record of Service   244

     Squadron Posting and Assignments   248

     Honours and Awards   248

     Bishop's Confirmed Victories   249

   The Top British Aces, 1914–18   252

   Leading Allied Aces   255

   Leading Enemy Aces   258

   Aeroplanes Flown by Bishop in
     World War I   259

   Aircraft Specifications and Data   260

LIST OF ILLUSTRATIONS

Major William A. Bishop

Bishop standing next to his favourite Nieuport 17

Lieutenant Bishop wearing the "O" and single wing
of an RFC Observer

Bishop's post-war partner, Billy Barker, right, about to
take the Prince of Wales for a flight during World
War I

A Nieuport 17 in flight over the lines

An SE-5A, British-built scout of the type flown by
Bishop

The famous Sopwith "Camel," contemporary of the
SE-5A

"The Red Baron" — Rittmeister Manfred von Richthofen — was the leading ace of both sides with eighty
confirmed victories. Like Bishop, he too entered the
war as a cavalry officer

The enemy Albatross D-V

The Fokker D-VII, probably the greatest plane to come
out of the war. Bishop tried his hand on a captured
one, like this

Aerial view of the Ypres battlefield

APPENDIX ILLUSTRATIONS

Fig. 1. Royal Flying Corps badge (top); RFC uniform button (bottom)

Fig. 2. RFC observer's wing insignia worn by Bishop

Fig. 3. Royal Canadian Air Force badge (top); Royal Air Force badge (bottom)

Fig. 4. British cockade or roundel

Fig. 5. Nieuport 17, three-view diagram

Fig. 6. SE-5A, three-view diagram

Fig. 7. Sopwith Triplane, three-view diagram

Fig. 8. Sopwith Camel, three-view diagram

Fig. 9. Pfalz D-III, three-view diagram

Fig. 10. Pfalz D-XII, three-view diagram

Fig. 11. Albatross D-V, three-view diagram

Fig. 12. Halberstadt CL-II, three-view diagram

Fig. 13. Hannoveraner CL-III, three-view diagram

Fig. 14. Aviatik C-II, three-view diagram

Fig. 15. Rumpler C-V, three-view diagram

INTRODUCTION

In writing this introduction to Billy Bishop's classic *Winged Warfare* I feel very much like the toastmaster introducing the great man for whom no introduction is really necessary. I wasn't born until four years after the close of the First World War (in which my father also participated as a second lieutenant with General Pershing's American Expeditionary Force in France), but Billy Bishop, along with my dad, were my boyhood heroes. His exploits and aerial duels above the clouds fired my imagination.

Oh yes, Billy Bishop had some of the human frailties, but nevertheless he was a great man. To me, he was a knight in shining armour who sallied forth daily to perform feats of valour and do battle with the enemy. Together with René Fonck, Jim McCudden, Eddie Rickenbacker, and the other white knights of King Arthur's Round Table, Bishop defeated the black knights led by Manfred von Richthofen, Ernst Udet, Werner Voss, and Hermann Goering (the last of whom went on to become, by far, the blackest knight of them all).

What sort of fellow was my "white knight"? What was his background?

Though a Canadian, Billy Bishop's boyhood was very much like that of any American boy who grew up in the Midwest or plains states during the same period. The similarity between that area and the middle Canadian provinces is remarkably close. Like any youth of high spirit and with a good sense of humour young Billy got into his share of troubles. As a cadet in the Royal Military College he ran afoul of authority there. But the war was on and he received the King's Commission as a Cavalry officer.

Once in France, Lieutenant Bishop found that he didn't care too much for life in the cavalry. He looked to the sky and was inspired by the thought of flight in the clean free air. Before not too long Bishop's transfer came through to the Royal Flying Corps (RFC). Unfortunately, his training gave little indication or promise of his future formidable ability as a fighter pilot. In fact he succeeded in demolishing a couple of British aircraft rather than German ones, and was about to be "washed out" as a flyer. As always, however, the customary Bishop luck prevailed. The RFC sorely needed pilots and the colonel gave him one more chance. Needless to say, Bishop made it.

His dash and daring gave the Allies one of their top fighter aces who participated in more than 170 air battles and emerged with seventy-two confirmed victories to his credit.

His career did not end here, however. Billy Bishop served his country again in World War II as Marshal of the Royal Canadian Air Force (RCAF), and his son fought as a fighter pilot in one of its squadrons.

Billy Bishop is an all-time great, one of that fabulous contingent of First World War Canadian aces that included his close friend and post-war business partner, Billy

14

Barker; Ray Collishaw, leader of the famed Naval Black Flight; and Roy Brown, credited with shooting down the Red Baron von Richthofen.

Such were the exploits that fired my childish flights of fancy. And they were encouraged by such pulp paper magazines as *Sky Birds, Flying Aces, War Birds,* and *G-2 Battle Aces.* They were enhanced even more by such dramatic motion picture classics as *Hell's Angels* and *Dawn Patrol.* My appetite was further whetted by trading cards—the same kind that kids collect today. They came with a packet of chewing gum and had pictures of the World War I aces and their aircraft, instead of baseball players. We used to toss for them and swap them.

"Hey, I'll give you a Rickenbacker and a Fokker D-VII for a Bishop!"

Probably our closest contact to that ultimate thrill of flying came with the building of model aeroplanes—models of the Spad, Albatross, Sopwith Camel, Pfalz, Nieuport, SE-5, etc. But these weren't the highly detailed, perfectly scaled, pre-moulded plastic models, or the petrol engine, electrically controlled flying models the kids have today. Oh no, not by a long shot. Our non-flying or solid display models were shaped by hand (ours), and a sharp knife, from a square block of balsa wood, and the wings, tail surfaces, rudder, struts, etc. were cut out with a razor blade from flat sheets of balsa wood. Our flying models were powered solely by rubber bands.

Looking back over the years, the United States has fought three major wars in this century, excluding the Vietnam fracas. The aeroplane first saw action in World War I and it was developed and honed to a fine degree during the four years of that war. The improvements made during this period gave rise to the great aviation and space industry we know today. Basic and crude as these wood and canvas aircraft were by comparison with today's standards, there is no denying that aerial combat in the First World War was more colourful, at least as far as the non-participants on the sidelines were concerned, than World War II and the Korean conflict.

Let's face it, by the end of World War I the Spad XIII flew at a top speed of 120 miles per hour in level flight. Other Allied and opposing German aircraft flew at comparable speeds or had other advantages of manoeuvrability to make up for their speed deficiency. When facing each other in combat an SE-5 could dive from out of the sun on to the tail of his Albatross adversary and if he didn't succeed in downing him on that pass could climb again and hit him from below. And the battle would continue in an ever-tightening circle, with each one trying to get on to the tail of the other manoeuvring to "draw a bead on him," or loop up and over to get behind his opponent. They faked stalls and simulated spirals, as though crashing to earth, to shake a persistent foe.

These fabulous early fighter planes moved at a speed that enabled them to stick with a protagonist and continue the battle until one was shot down or broke off contact and lit for home.

The World War II Thunderbolts, Spitfires, and Mustangs tore at the Me 109s and Focke Wulf 190s at speeds approaching 400 mph. Their ability to remain with an adversary in a "dog fight" was severely limited by the excessive speed of the aircraft. Such manoeuvring became impos-

16

sible in the first jet war—in the skies over Korea where F-86 Sabrejets and Mig 15s tangled, attaining speeds of 600 mph in level flight where a single pass took the planes miles apart.

Any personal relationship between opposing flyers that might have existed in World War I was lost forever. No longer would a fighter pilot fly over the enemy's aerodrome and drop a note challenging him to an aerial duel. Nor would the victor in battle fly over the lines to drop flowers as a salute to his fallen foe.

Those days of gallantry in battle and high adventure come alive again in Billy Bishop's *Winged Warfare*. Here, in his own colourful words, is the exciting firsthand account of the British Empire's great fighter ace of the First World War.

STANLEY M. ULANOFF

WINGED WARFARE

An Air Combat Classic

CHAPTER 1

IT WAS THE MUD, I think, that made me take to flying. I had fully expected that going into battle would mean for me the saddle of a galloping charger, instead of the snug little cock-pit of a modern aeroplane. The mud, on a certain day in July 1915, changed my whole career in the war.

We were in England. I had gone over as an officer of the Mississauga Horse, of Toronto, a cavalry detachment of the Second Canadian Division. It had rained for days in torrents, and there was still a drizzle coming down as I set out for a tour of the horse-lines.

Ordinary mud is bad enough, when you have to make your home in it, but the particular brand of mud that infests a cavalry camp has a meanness all its own. Everything was dank, and slimy, and boggy. I had succeeded in getting myself mired to the knees when suddenly, from somewhere out of the storm, appeared a trim little aeroplane.

It landed hesitatingly in a near-by field as if scorning to brush its wings against so sordid a landscape; then away again up into the clean grey mists.

How long I stood there gazing into the distance I do not know, but when I turned to slog my way back through the mud my mind was made up. I knew there was only one place to be on such a day—up above the clouds and in the summer sunshine. I was going into the battle that way. I was going to meet the enemy in the air.

I had never given much thought to being a soldier, even after my parents had sent me to the Royal Military College at Kingston, when I was seventeen years of age. I will say for my parents that they had not thought much of me as a professional soldier either. But they did think, for some reason or other, that a little military discipline at the Royal Military College would do me a lot of good— and I suppose it did.

In any event, those three years at the R.M.C. stood me in good stead when the rush came in Canada, when everywhere, everybody was doing his best to get taken on in some capacity in order to get to the front quickly.

We Canadians will never forget the thrill of those first days of the war, and then the terrible waiting before most of us could get to the other side. Our great fear was that the fighting would all be over before we could give a hand in it. How little we knew then of the glory that was to be Canada's in the story of the Western Front, of the sacrifices that were to reach to nearly every fireside in the Dominion!

For many months my bit seemed to consist of training, more training, delays and more delays. But at last we got over. We crossed in an old-time cattle-boat. Oh, what a trip! Fifteen days to reach England! We had 700 horses on board, and 700 seasick horses are not the most congenial steamer company.

We were very proud to be in England. We felt we were really in the war-zone, and soon would be in the fighting. But it is a great mistake to think that when you sail from

America you are going to burst right up to the front and go over the top at daybreak in the morning. The way to the war is long. There was more work and more training for us in England. At first we were sent to a very sandy camp on the coast, and from there to a very muddy camp somewhere else in the British Isles.

It was to this camp that the aeroplane came that stormy day in July. A week later my plans were in motion. I met a friend in the Royal Flying Corps and confided in him my ambition to fly. He assured me it would be easy to arrange a transfer, and instructed me as to what I should do. If I wanted to get to the front quickly I would have to go as an observer, meaning that when I flew over the German lines I would be the "passenger" in a two-seated plane and would do just what my title indicated—observe.

If one has a stomach for flying, it doesn't take long to become a fairly competent observer. There are observer schools where they teach you just what to observe and what not to observe. This is not a joke. If an observer lets his gaze wander to too many non-essentials he cannot do the real observing that is expected of him.

A few more days of cavalry mud and I was convinced that to be an observer in the air was far better than commanding a division on the ground. So I applied for my transfer, got it, and went to an observing school. I loved those first few flights in an old training "bus." I don't think she could make more than fifty miles an hour; and as for climbing, she struggled and shook and gasped like a freight train going up a mountain side. But it was thrilling enough for me in those days, despite the fact that I soon began to envy the pilot who had all the fun of running the machine and could make it do a few lame and decrepit stunts.

After a few months I was graduated as an observer and was awarded my first insignia of the Flying Corps—an O, with one outstretched wing attached to it, to be worn on the left breast of the tunic. I was rather proud of that one wing, but more determined than ever to win the double wings of a fully fledged pilot, and some day have a machine of my own.

In a very short time I was in France and ready for my first trip over the enemy lines. As I look back upon it now my life as an observer seems very tame. The work of the reconnaissance and artillery machines, as well as the photography and bombing planes, is very important. It goes on day and night, in good weather and bad, but all the times I was observing I wanted to be fighting. Whenever I saw one of the small, swift, single-seater machines, which were just coming into vogue then for fighting purposes, my resolves to become a fighting pilot would grow stronger and stronger.

But far be it from me to detract one iota from the work of the observers. They take enormous risks and seldom get any of the glory. The men in the Corps recognize and appreciate the quality of their work, but the public at large rarely hears of them. The feats of the fighting planes form the spectacular and fascinating side of flying, but in a sense the daily drudgery of the bombers, the photographers, and the observers is of even greater value to the fighting men on the ground.

It is no child's play to circle above a German battery observing for half an hour or more, with your machine tossing about in air, tortured by exploding shells and black shrapnel puffballs coming nearer and nearer to you like the ever-extending finger-tips of some giant hand of death. But it is just a part of the never-ceasing war. In the air service this work is never done. Everywhere along the line the big guns wait daily for the wireless touch of aeroplanes to set them booming at targets carefully selected from a previous day of observation. Big shells cannot be wasted. The human effort involved in creating them and placing them beside the well-screened guns at the front is far too great for that.

Every shell must be watched. It is a startling thing, but true. When we possess the high ground and the ridges, it is not always necessary for the aeroplanes or the balloons to do the observing; the artillery observing officers can go forward on the ground and from a convenient tree-top, a bit of trench, or a sheltering shell-hole see exactly what his guns are doing.

Every day there are hundreds of photographs to be taken, so that the British map-makers can trace each detail of the German trench positions and can check any changes in the enemy zone. Information is to be gained at all times by all manner of reconnaissances—some of them carrying you fifty to sixty miles in the enemy country. Then, there is the fighting patrol work which goes on all hours. The patrol is not on our side of the line. It is far over the German lines to keep the enemy machines from coming too close even to their own front trenches. Of course they do slip over occasionally, but more than often have to pay for their temerity.

The British infantryman—Mr. Tommy Atkins—takes it

as a personal insult to have a Hun machine flying over him. It shouldn't be done, he says, and he grouses about it for weeks. How different with the German infantryman! Our planes are on top of them most of the time. The Huns used to write wrathful letters home about it. Sometimes our infantry has captured these letters before they were posted, and they used to amuse us when we got them in the daily army reports. I remember one particularly peevish old Boche who wrote last May:

"The air activity where we are is very great. The English will soon be taking the very caps off our heads."

It is great fun to fly very low along the German trenches and give them a burst of machine-gun bullets as a greeting in the morning, or a good-night salute in the evening. They don't like it a bit. But we love it; we love to see the Kaiser's proud Prussians running for cover like so many rats.

Whatever your mission, whether it is to direct artillery fire, to photograph, to bomb an ammunition-dump or supply-train, or just to look old Fritz over and see in a general way what he is up to, your first journey into Hunland is a memorable event in your life. I may say here, in passing, that in the Flying Corps a German is seldom anything but a Hun, and the territory back of his lines is seldom anything but Hunland. Our general orders tell us to designate a Hun plane as an "enemy aircraft" in our reports, or "E.A." for short, but, nevertheless, we always think of both the machine and the pilot as a Hun, and they will ever be.

If it is artillery work you are on, you have learned to send down signals to your battery by means of a wireless buzzer, and you are equipped with intricate zone maps that enable you to pick out all manner of fixed objects in the enemy's domain. You can locate his dug-outs, his dumps, his lines of communication, his battery positions, his shelters behind the trees, and, in a general way, keep tab on his "ways that are dark, and tricks that are vain."

The day for your trip over happens to be one of wondrous sunshine and the clearest possible visibility. At every aerodrome behind the long British war-line the aeroplanes are out of their hangars, and are being tested with such a babel of noisy explosions that in moving about with a companion you have fairly to shout to make yourself heard. With your pilot you climb into the waiting two-seater. It has been groomed for the day and fussed over with as much care as a mother might bestow upon her only offspring starting for Sunday school.

"Contact, sir?" questions a mechanic standing at the propeller.

"Contact," repeats the pilot.

There is a click of the electric ignition switch, the propeller is given a sharp swing over, and the engine starts with a roar. Once or twice there is a cough, but pretty soon she is "hitting" just right on every one of her multiple cylinders. It is all the mechanics can do to hold her back. Then the pilot throttles down to a very quiet little purr and signals to the attendants to draw away the chocks from under the wheels. Slowly you move forward under your own "steam" and "taxi" across the field rather bumpily, to head her into the wind. This accomplished, the throttle is opened wide, you rush forward with increasing speed, you feel the tail of the machine leave the ground, and then you go leaping into space.

You climb in great wide circles above the aerodrome, rig up the wireless, send a few test signals, get back the correct responses, and arrange your maps, while the pilot, with one eye on his instruments and the other on familiar landmarks, sets sail for the German lines, gaining height all the while. On the way to the lines you pass over your battery and send wireless word that you are ready to "carry on." It is to be a day of "counter-battery" work, which means that some of our batteries are going to "do in" some of the Hun batteries. The modern guns of war are very temperamental and restless. They get tired of firing at infantry trenches and roads and things, and more often go to shooting at each other. In this you help them all you can.

And now you come to make the acquaintance of "Archie," who will pursue you through all your flying-days at the front. "Archie" is a presumptuous person and takes the liberty of speaking first.

"Woof! Woof!" he barks out. Then—"Hiss-s-s. Bang! Bang!" Two flashes of crimson fire, and two swirling patches of black smoke jump out of the air a hundred yards or so in front of you.

The experienced pilot swerves a little neatly and avoids the next volley, which breaks far to your right. "Archie" keeps barking at you for quite a while and you seem to be leaving a perfect trail of the diffusing black smoke-balls in your wake. The pilot looks back at you and grins; he wonders if you have the "wind up"—army talk for being scared to death. It isn't any disgrace to get the

28

"wind up" at the war, and there are few of us who can truthfully say we haven't had a queerish sort of feeling every now and then.

"Archie," of course, is an anti-aircraft cannon. How the airmen first happened to name him "Archibald" I do not know; it was when we got to know him better, and fear him less, that we began to call him "Archie." With "Archie" it is the old story of familiarity breeding contempt, but of late the German "Archie" family has multiplied to such an extent as almost to make it dangerous to go visiting across the Hun lines. The German shrapnel shells are nearly always mixed with high-explosive. They are very noisy, but most of the time your engine is making such clatter the explosive efforts to wing you in flight go entirely unnoticed.

Leaving the border-guarding "Archies" far behind, you fly on until you pick up the four mounds that indicate the German battery position. You fly rather low to get a good look at it. The Huns generally know what your coming means and they prepare to take cover. You return a little way toward your own lines and signal to your battery to fire. In a moment you see the flash of a big gun. Then nothing seems to happen for an eternity. As a matter of fact twenty to thirty seconds elapse and then fifty yards beyond the German battery you see a spurt of grey-black earth spring from the ground. You signal a correction of the range. The next shot goes fifty yards short. In artillery language you have "bracketed" your target. You again signal a correction, giving a range just in between the first two shots. The next shell that goes over explodes in a gun-pit.

"Good shooting," you signal to the battery, "carry on"—particular battery is silenced for good and all. "Archie" tries for you again as you return across the lines, but his range-finding is very bad to-day. You salute your battery as you sail over, then land a few minutes later at the aerodrome well satisfied with your three hours' work.

You have been to Hunland, and you feel your career in the air has really begun.

CHAPTER 2

ALTOGETHER I SPENT four months in France as an observer. How I longed during all that time for a fight in the air! But no real chances came, and, finally, I quitted my seat as a passenger without having fired a single combat shot from the tidy little machine gun that was always near me and seemed to yearn as much as I did to have a go at the enemy.

I injured my knee after an observing trip one day, when the pilot crashed the machine in landing; and while I did not have to go to hospital with it, it gradually grew worse until May 1916, when I had to lay up several months for repairs.

My sick-leave over, I reported for duty again and got a real surprise—I was told I could learn to fly! This made me happier than I can express. I pictured myself in one of the swift little fighting planes I had seen in France, and I felt in my heart of hearts that I would make good. I already knew what it felt like to fly; I knew the language of the air, the esprit of the Corps, and some of the heart-palpitating peculiarities of our best-balanced engines. But all this time I had been a sort of innocent bystander. Now, at last, I was going into the air "on my own."

The first step was to go to a school of instruction—a ground school—where the theory of flying and the mechanical side of aviation are expounded to you. I went through these courses, and by special permission was allowed to take my examination three weeks earlier than would have been the case in the ordinary course of events. I worked like a Trojan, and passed without much difficulty. Then was to come the real part of it all, the part for which I had waited for over a year.

On November 1st, 1916, I was sent to another school for elementary training in the air. This consisted, first of all, in going up in another old machine—a steady type called the Maurice Farman, and fitted with a dual set of controls, so that the instructor could manage one while I tried to manage the other. Never will I forget those days of dual control. I tried very hard, but seemed to me I just could not get the proper "feel" of the machine. First the instructor would tell me I was "ham-handed"—that I gripped the controls too tightly with every muscle tense. After that I would get what you might call timid-handed, and not hold the controls tightly enough. My instructor and I both suffered tortures. So when suddenly one day he told me I could go up alone, I had my doubts as to whether it was confidence or desperation that dictated his decision. I didn't worry long as to which it was; I was willing to take the chance.

Then followed my first solo! This is, I think, the greatest day in a flying man's life. Certainly I did not stop talking about it for the next three weeks at least. I felt a great and tender pity for all the millions of people in the world who never have a chance to do a solo!

An ambulance stood in the aerodrome, and it seemed to me, as it has to many another student-pilot, that all the other business of flying had suddenly ceased so that everybody could look at me. I noticed with a shiver that the ambulance had its engine running. Were the doctors at the hospital expectantly fondling their knives? Everybody looked cold-blooded and heartless. But I had to do it: so into the machine I crawled, trying to look cheerful, but feeling awfully lonesome. How I got off the ground I do not know, but once in the air it was not nearly so bad—not much worse than the first time you started downhill on an old-fashioned bicycle.

I wasn't taking any liberties. I flew as straight ahead as I could, climbing steadily all the time. But at last I felt I had to turn, and I tried a very slow, gradual one, not wanting to bank either too steeply or too little. They told me afterward I did some remarkable skidding on that turn, but I was blissfully ignorant of a little detail like that and went gaily on my way. I banked a little more on my next turn and didn't skid so much.

For a time I felt very much pleased with myself circling above the aerodrome, but suddenly an awful thought came to me. Somehow or other I had to get that machine down to the earth again. How blissful it would be if I could just keep on flying! At last, however, I screwed up all my courage, reached for the throttle, pushed it back, and the engine almost stopped. I knew the next thing to do was to put her nose down. So down it went at a steep angle. I felt it was too steep, so I pulled her nose up a bit, then put it down again, and in a series of steps I had been told carefully to carry out, descended toward the ground.

About forty feet from the ground, however, I did everything I had been told to do when two feet from the ground. So I made a perfect landing—only forty feet too high.

Eventually I realized this slight error, and down went her nose again. We rapidly got nearer the ground, and then I repeated my perfect landing—about eight feet up. This time I just sat and suffered, while the now thoroughly exasperated old machine, taking matters into its own hands, dropped with a "plonk" the intervening distance. There was no damage, because the training-machines are built for such work, and can stand all sorts of hard knocks.

After doing my first solo, I progressed rather rapidly, and in a few days was passed on to a higher instruction squadron and began to fly more warlike machines. I found that to qualify as a pilot I had to pass certain tests in night flying. This awed me to a certain extent, but it also appealed to me, for just two months before the first Zeppelins had been brought down at night on English soil by our airmen. I was very anxious to get taken on for this work, and eventually succeeded.

Night flying is a fearsome thing—but tremendously interesting. Anyone who has ever been swimming at night will appreciate what I mean. All the familiar objects and landmarks, that seem so friendly by day, become weird and repellent monsters at night. It is simple enough to go up in the dark, and simple enough to sail away. But it is quite something else to come down again without taking off a chimney-pot or "strafing" a big oak tree. The landing tests are done with the help of flares on the ground. My first flight at night had most of the thrills of my first solo. I "taxied" out to what I thought a good place to take-off from. The instructor shouted a few last words to me above the noise of the motor. I turned the machine to face down the long line of lights, opened out the engine, raced along the ground, then plunged up into utter blackness.

I held the controls very carefully and kept my eyes glued to the instruments that gleamed brightly under little electric bulbs inside the machine. I could not see a thing around me; only the stars overhead. Underneath there was a great black void. After flying straight forwards for several minutes I summoned up courage enough to make a turn. I carefully and gradually rounded the corner, and then away off to one side I could see the flares on the ground. I completed a big circuit and shut off the engine preparatory to landing. Suddenly, in the midst of my descent, I realized I had misjudged it very badly, so quickly put the engine on again and proceeded to fly around a second time. Then I came down, and, to my intense surprise, made quite a good landing. This was only the beginning. I had to repeat the trick several times.

On the final test I had to attain a given height. I left the ground as before, and just as I did so could see the reflection of the flares on the tin roofs of our huts. It made a great impression upon me, as I climbed away into the darkness. Then my thoughts went to my engine and I realized it was as important as my own heart. I listened to its steady beat with an anxious ear. Once or twice there was a slight kick or hitch in its smooth rhythm. No matter how many cylinders you have whirring in front of you, the instant one misses your heart hears it even before your ears do. Several times my heart seemed to stop. The tension became very great as I toiled and struggled up through the night. The lack of anything upon which I

35

could put my eyes outside the machine gave me a very queer feeling.

One other machine was up at the same time, doing its test, and somehow, although the space in the air is very wide, I had a great fear that we might collide, so I gazed anxiously out into the darkness trying to see the little navigation lights we carried on our wings. It is hard to look into jet blackness, and the strain hurt my eyes, but I was afraid not to look for all I was worth. I continued to fly as far as possible in a dead straight line. When-ever I had to make a turn I made a very gradual one, hardly daring to bank, or tilt, my machine at all. It is funny, this feeling at night that you must not bank, and a most dangerous instinct to follow. The feeling that you are off an even keel upsets you, as you have no horizon or apparent ground below you to take your bearings by, and you have to go by the instruments, or tell from the "feel" of the machine itself, whether you are level or not.

However, at the stage of learning I had reached I knew nothing of the real feel of a machine and was entirely dependent upon the instruments. This is not a very reassuring state of mind, so when the instruments at last indicated I had attained the required height, it was with a happy heart that I throttled back my engine to come down. I was afraid to shut it completely off for fear that it would get too cold to pick up when I put it on again. When you come down with your engine running it takes a much longer time to reach the ground. Every thousand feet or so, as I lost height, I would carefully try out the engine, and do a complete circuit. Underneath me I could see the little twinkling flares, and kept them in sight as much as possible on the downward journey to make certain of not losing myself. Finally, I reached the ground and made a careful landing.

When I stepped out of the machine I had at last qualified as a pilot. I was sent to a home-defence squadron near the mouth of the Thames. I spent hours practising in the air both by day and by night. Several times we had flight manœuvres at night, and that was ticklish work. We would go up to patrol a certain area with lights showing on all the aerodromes in that section of the country, so that you could steer by them. I don't know of many greater tests of a pilot's skill than this flying in the dark, with a lot of machines about you in the air, their little navigation lights looking for all the world like so many moving stars. The cold of the higher altitudes at night is agonizingly intense. After half an hour or so in the frigid zone you get sort of numb and then for a long while the cold doesn't seem to affect you any more. The real nasty part is when you have landed and begin to thaw out. It is really worse than the original freezing.

In spite of the discomforts and the dangers of night flying you could not fail to admire the great beauty of the scene below you when the lights were on and sparkling. These lights would mean nothing to a stranger, but to us in the air they were friendly beacons of safety and gave us a feeling of absolute security. On such nights the skies would seem full to overflowing with myriad stars. We finally became so accustomed to flying in the dark that nothing troubled us except ground mists or light fogs that would occasionally slip in from the sea, obliterate the lights, and make landing a difficult and perilous task.

My luck as a Zeppelin hunter was very poor. I used to

dream occasionally about stalking the great monsters in the high thin air, pouring a drum of blazing bullets into them and gloating as they flared into flame. But no real Zeppelins ever came my way. The cold nights that we stood by on duty waiting for them were very long, but not without their compensations. There would be two of us at a given station. We would play cards, strum on some sort of instrument, read for an hour or so, play cards again, and all the while hoping for an alarm that would send us aloft in pursuit of a marauding gasbag from over the sea.

Christmas Day we cooked our own turkey and the rest of the meal. Then, in a burst of Yuletide hospitality, we telephoned to a local hotel and told the manager to send anybody he wanted to out to the aerodrome for dinner. Alas for our ten-pound turkey! The guests from the hotel kept coming until there were actually twenty of them. However, in some miraculous way, we managed to feed the hungry score. Having partaken of our food, they did not tarry long. Night shut in early and once more we took up our wintry vigil.

Toward the end of February word came through from the War Office one night that I was to go to France. I had become convinced that the winter would not offer much opportunity at Zeppelin hunting, and had applied several times for duty at the fighting front. Before I went, however, there was another course at a special school, where I learned to fly the smallest of our single-seater machines. Now, I felt, I had reached the height of my ambition at last; actually to fly one of these tiny, wasp-like fighting machines seemed to me the most wonderful thing in the

38

world. A few days later, when I reported for my orders to cross the Channel it was with a gay heart, and a determination to reflect as much honour as I could upon the double wings on my left breast.

CHAPTER 3

WITH A DOZEN other flying men I landed at Boulogne on March 7th, 1917, for my second go at the war. At the Boulogne quay we separated, and I wish I could say that "some flew east and some flew west," but as a matter of fact we didn't fly at all. Instead, we meandered along over the slow French railroads for nearly two days before reaching our destinations.

One other pilot and myself had been ordered to join a flying squadron on the southern sector of the British line. The squadron to which we were assigned had a great reputation, one of the best in all France, and we were very proud to become members of it. Captain Albert Ball, who was resting in England at the time, but who came back to France in the late spring and was killed within a few weeks, had brought down twenty-nine Hun machines as a member of "our" squadron. That was an inspiration in itself.

The first day of my stay with the squadron there was no flying, and so I wandered about the field hangars looking at the machines. They were all of a type I had never seen before at close range—Nieuport Scouts, very small and, of course, with but a single seat. Being a French model, the Nieuport Scout is a beautiful creature. The distinctly British machines—and some of our newer ones are indeed marvels of the air—are built strictly for business, with no particular attention paid to the beauty of lines. The French, however, never overlook such things.

The modern fighting scout—and to my mind the single-seater is the only real aeroplane for offensive work—may have the power of 200 horses throbbing in its wonderful engine. Some of the machines are very slender of waist and almost transparent of wing. Aeroplanes do not thrust their war-like nature upon the casual observer. One has to look twice before definitely locating the gun or guns attached so unobtrusively to the frame-work, and synchronized, where necessary, to shoot through the whirring propeller in front. Such guns are connected to the engine itself by means of cams, and are so arranged that they can fire only when the propeller reaches a given position, thus allowing the bullets to pass safely between the blades. It seems like a very delicate bit of timing, but the devices are extremely simple.

The nacelle, or cock-pit, of the modern machine, I have heard people say, suggests to them the pilot-house of a palatial private yacht in miniature. They are generally finished in hard wood and there are polished nickel instruments all about you. They indicate height, speed, angle, revolutions, and almost everything an airman ought to know. There are ingenious sights for the guns and range-finders for bomb-dropping. When he is tucked away in the nacelle, a little well-like compartment, about as big as an ordinary barrel, only the pilot's head is visible above the freeboard of the body of the machine—the body being technically known as the fuselage. Directly in front of the pilot is a little glass wind-screen, a sort of half-moon effect.

We newcomers at the squadron—the other pilot and myself—had to stand by the next day and watch the patrols leaving to do their work over the lines. It was thrilling even to us, accustomed as we were to ordinary flying, to see the trim little fighters take the air, one after the other, circle above the aerodrome, and then, dropping into a fixed formation, set their courses to the east. That night we listened with eager ears to the discussion of a fight in which a whole patrol had been engaged. We stay-at-homes had spent the day practise-flying in the new machines. There were three days more of this for me, and then, having passed some standard tests to show my familiarity with the Nieuport type, I was told the next morning I was to cross the lines for the first time as the master of my own machine.

The squadron commander had been killed the day before I arrived from England, and the new one arrived the day after. It rather pleased and in a sense comforted me to know that the new commander was also going over in a single-seater for the first time when I did. He had been flying up to this time a two-seater machine which calls for entirely different tactics during a fight. Two-seater machines, as a rule, have guns that can be turned about in different positions. On the fighting scouts they generally are rigidly fixed. This means that it is necessary to aim the machine at anything you wish to fire at.

The night before I was to "go over" I received my orders. I was to bring up the rear of a flight of six machines, and I assure you it was *some* task bringing up the rear of that formation. I had my hands full from the very start. It seemed to me my machine was slower than the rest, and as I wasn't any too well acquainted with it, I had a great time trying to keep my proper place, and to keep the others

43

from losing me. I was so busy at the task of keeping up that my impressions of outside things were rather vague. Every time the formation turned or did anything unexpected, it took me two or three minutes to get back in my proper place. But I got back every time as fast as I could. I felt safe when I was in the formation and scared when I was out of it, for I had been warned many times that it is a fatal mistake to get detached and become a straggler. And I had heard of the German "head-hunters," too. They are German machines that fly very high and avoid combat with anything like an equal number, but are quick to pounce down upon a straggler, or an Allied machine that has been damaged and is bravely struggling to get home. Fine sportsmanship, that!

The way I clung to my companions that day reminded me of some little child hanging to its mother's skirts while crossing a crowded street. I remember I also felt like a child does when it is going up a dark flight of stairs, and is sure something is going to reach out of somewhere and grab it. I was so intent on the clinging part that I paid very little attention to anything else.

We climbed to a height of more than two miles on our side of the lines, then crossed them. There were other formations of machines in the air, patrolling at various places. I could see them in the distance, but for the life of me I could not tell whether they were friendly or hostile. On the chance that they might be the latter, I clung closer than ever to my comrades. Then, a long way off, I was conscious that a fight was going on between a patrol of our machines and a Hun formation. I could make little of it all until finally I saw what seemed like a dark ball of smoke falling, and learned afterwards it was one of our own machines going down in flames, having been shot and set on fire by the enemy airmen.

A few minutes after this my attention was attracted elsewhere. Our old friends the "Archies" were after us. It is no snug billet, this being in the rear of a formation when the "Archies" are giving a show. They always seem to aim at the leading machine, but come closer to hitting the one at the end of the procession. The first shot I heard fired was a terrific "bang" close to my ears. I felt the tail of my machine suddenly shoot up into the air, and I fell about 300 feet before I managed completely to recover control. That shot, strange to relate, was the closest I have ever had from anti-aircraft fire. The smoke from the exploding shell enveloped me. But close as it was, only one piece of the flying steel fragments hit my machine. Even that did no damage at all.

After recovering control I looked about hastily for the rest of my formation, and discovered that by now they were at least half a mile away, and somewhat higher than I was. Terrified at being left alone, I put my engine on full and, by taking a short cut, managed to catch up with them. Much relieved, I fell in under the formation, feeling safe again, and not so alone in the world.

We continued to patrol our beat, and I was keeping my place so well I began to look about a bit. After one of these gazing spells, I was startled to discover that the three leading machines of our formation were missing. Apparently they had disappeared into nothingness. I looked around hastily, and then discovered them underneath me, diving rapidly. I didn't know just what they were diving at, but I

45

dived, too. Long before I got down to them, however, they had been in a short engagement half a mile below me, and had succeeded in frightening off an enemy artillery machine which had been doing wireless observation work. It was a large white German two-seater, and I learned after we landed that it was a well-known machine and was commonly called "the flying pig." Our patrol leader had to put up with a lot of teasing that night because he had attacked the "pig." It seems that it worked every day on this part of the front, was very old, had a very bad pilot, and a very poor observer to protect him.

It was a sort of point of honour in the squadron that the decrepit old "pig" should not actually be shot down. It was considered fair sport, however, to frighten it. Whenever our machines approached, the "pig" would begin a series of clumsy turns and ludicrous manœuvres, and would open a frightened fire from ridiculously long ranges. The observer was a very bad shot and never succeeded in hitting any of our machines, so attacking this particular German was always regarded more as a joke than a serious part of warfare. The idea was only to frighten the "pig," but our patrol leader had made such a determined dash at him the first day we went over, that he never appeared again. For months the patrol leader was chided for playing such a nasty trick upon a harmless old man.

During my dive after the three forward machines, I managed to lose them and the enemy machine as well. So I turned and went up again, where I found two of my companions. We flew around looking for the others, but could not find them, so continued the patrol until our time was up and then returned to the aerodrome. The missing ones arrived about the same time and reported they had had a great many fights, but no decisive ones.

About this time the Germans were beginning in earnest their famous retreat from the country of the Somme. There had been days upon days of heavy fogs and flying had been impossible. A few machines went up from time to time, but could see nothing. The wily old Hun had counted upon these thick days to shield his well-laid plans, and made the most of them. Finally, there came a strong breeze from the south-west that swept the fog away and cleared the ground of all mist and haze. This was on that wonderfully clear March day just before the Germans evacuated Bapaume and left it a mass of ruins. We were early in the air, and had no sooner reached our proper height to cross the lines than we could see something extraordinary was happening behind the German trenches. From 15,000 feet we could see for miles and miles around. The ground was a beautiful green and brown, and slightly to the south we could see the shell-pitted battlefields of the Somme, each shell-hole with glistening water in it.

A few miles to the east there were long streaks of white smoke. Soon we realized that the Germans had set fire to scores of villages behind their front. From where we flew we could see between fifty and sixty of them ablaze. The long smoke-plumes blowing away to the north-east made one of the most beautiful ground-pictures I have ever seen from an aeroplane, but at the same time I was enraged beyond words. It had affected every pilot in the patrol the same way. We flew up and down over this burning country for two hours hunting, and wishing for German machines to come up and fight, but none appeared. We returned at last to the aerodrome and told what we had seen during our patrol, but news of the fires had long since been reported by the airmen whose duty it is to look out for such things, and our General Staff at once had surmised the full import of what was happening.

The next week was full of exciting adventures. For days the clouds hung at very low altitudes, seldom being higher than 4000 feet, and of course it was necessary for us to fly underneath them. At times during the famous retreat it was hard to tell just where the Germans were and where they were not. It was comparatively easy for the soldiers on the ground to keep in touch with the German rearguard by outpost fighting, but it was for us to keep tabs on the main bodies of troops. We would fly over a sector of country from east to west and mark down on our maps the points from which we were fired at. It was easy to know the Germans were at those particular points. This was very tense and exciting work, flying along very low and waiting each second to hear the rattle of machine guns or the crack of a shell. We were flaunting ourselves as much as possible over the German lines in order to draw their fire.

CHAPTER 4

ON MARCH 25TH came my first real fight in the air, and, as luck would have it, my first victory. The German retreat was continuing. Four of us were detailed to invade the enemy country, to fly low over the trenches, and in general to see what the Boche troops were doing and where they were located.

Those were very queer days. For a time it seemed that both armies—German and British alike—had simply dissolved. Skirmishes were the order of the day on the ground and in the air. The grim, fixed lines of battle had vanished for the time being, and the Germans were falling back to their famous Hindenburg positions.

The clouds had been hanging low as usual, but after we had flown well in advance of our old lines and into what had been so recently Hunland, the weather suddenly cleared. So we began to climb to more comfortable altitudes and finally reached about 9000 feet. We flew about for a long while without seeing anything, and then from the corner of my eye I spied what I believed to be three enemy machines. They were some distance to the east of us, and evidently were on patrol duty to prevent any of our pilots or observers getting too near the rapidly changing German positions. The three strange machines approached us, but our leader continued to fly straight ahead without altering his course in the slightest degree. Soon there was no

longer any doubt as to the identity of the three aircraft—
they were Huns, with the big, distinguishing black iron
crosses on their planes. They evidently were trying to surprise us, and we allowed them to approach, trying all the
time to appear as if we had not seen them.

Like nearly all other pilots who come face to face with a
Hun in the air for the first time, I could hardly realize that
these were real, live, hostile machines. I was fascinated by
them and wanted to circle about and have a good look at
them. The German Albatross machines are perfect beauties
to look upon. Their swept-back planes give them more of a
bird-like appearance than any other machines flying on the
western front. Their splendid, graceful lines lend to them
an effect of power and flying ability far beyond what they
really possess. After your first few experiences with enemy
machines at fairly close quarters you have very little trouble distinguishing them in the future. You learn to sense
their presence, and to know their nationality long before
you can make out the crosses on the planes.

Finally, the three enemy machines got behind us, and we
slowed down so that they would overtake us all the sooner.
When they had approached to about 400 yards, we opened
out our engines and turned. One of the other pilots, as well
as myself, had never been in a fight before, and we were
naturally slower to act than the other two. My first real
impression of the engagement was that one of the enemy
machines dived down, then suddenly came up again and
began to shoot at one of our people from the rear.

I had a quick impulse and followed it. I flew straight at
the attacking machine from a position where he could not
see me and opened fire. My "tracer" bullets—bullets that

50

show a spark and a thin little trail of smoke as they speed through the air—began at once to hit the enemy machine. A moment later the Hun turned over on his back and seemed to fall out of control. This was just at the time that the Germans were doing some of their famous falling stunts. Their machines seemed to be built to stand extraordinary strains in that respect. They would go spinning down from great heights, and just when you thought they were sure to crash, they would suddenly come under control, flatten out into correct flying position, and streak for the rear of their lines with every ounce of horse-power imprisoned in their engines.

When my man fell from his upside-down position into a spinning nose-dive, I dived after him. Down he went for a full thousand feet and then regained control. I had forgotten caution and everything else in my wild and overwhelming desire to destroy this thing that for the time being represented all of Germany to me. I could not have been more than forty yards behind the Hun when he flattened out, and again I opened fire. It made my heart leap to see my smoking bullets hitting the machine just where the closely hooded pilot was sitting. Again the Hun went into a dive and shot away from me vertically toward the earth.

Suspecting another ruse, and still unmindful of what might be happening to my companions in their set-to with the other Huns, I went into a wild dive after my particular opponent with my engine full on. With a machine capable of doing 110 to 120 miles an hour on the level, I must have attained 180 to 200 miles in that wrathful plunge. Meteor-like as was my descent, however, the Hun seemed to be falling faster still and got farther and farther away from me.

When I was still about 1500 feet up, he crashed into the ground below me. For a long time I had heard pilots speaking of "crashing" enemy machines, but I never fully appreciated the full significance of "crashed" until now. There is no other word for it.

I have not to this day fully analysed my feelings in those moments of my first victory. I don't think I fully realized what it all meant. When I pulled my machine out of its own somewhat dangerous dive, I suddenly became conscious of the fact that I had not the slightest idea in the world where I was. I had lost all sense of direction and distance; nothing had mattered to me except the shooting down of that enemy scout with the big black crosses that I shall never forget. Now I began to fear that I was well within the enemy country and that it was up to me to find some way of getting home. Then, to my dismay, I discovered that during our long dive my engine had filled up with lubricating oil and had stopped dead still. I tried every little trick I knew to coax a fresh start, but it was no use. I had no choice. I must land in the country directly beneath me, be it hostile or friendly. I turned in what seemed to me by instinct to be the way toward our own lines, and glided as far as I could without any help from the engine.

I saw beneath me a destroyed village, and my heart sank. I must be behind the German lines. Was my real flying career, just begun, to be ended so soon? Was I to suffer the fate the flying man most abhors—the helpless descent in Hunland and the meek submission to being taken prisoner? A hundred thoughts were racing through my head, but in a moment they were dispersed. It was that always ghastly rattle of a machine gun, firing at me from the ground. This left no doubt but that I was over enemy territory. I continued to glide, listlessly, toward the ground, not caring much now what the machine gun might do. My plight couldn't be much worse. I was convinced, in fact, that it couldn't possibly be worse. Mechanically, without realizing just what I was doing, but all the time following that first great instinct of self-preservation, I remember carefully picking out a clear path in the rough terrain beneath me, and making a last turn, I glided into it and landed.

Some hostile spirit within me made me seize the rocket pistol we used to fire signals with in the air—"Very" lights, they are called. What I expected to do with such an impotent weapon of offence or defence, I don't know, but it gave me a sort of armed feeling as I jumped out of the machine. I ran to a near-by ditch, following the irresistible battlefield impulse to "take cover." I lay for some time in the ditch waiting—waiting for my fate, whatever it was to be. Then I saw some people crawling toward me. They were anxious moments, and I had to rub my eyes two or three times before finally convincing myself that the oncoming uniforms were of muddy-brown and homely, if you will, but to me that day, khaki was the most wonderful, the most inspiring, the most soul-satisfying colour scheme ever beheld by the eyes of man. In an instant my whole life-outlook changed; literally it seemed to me that by some miracle I had come back from the land of the "missing."

The British "Tommies" had seen me land and had bravely crawled out to help me. They told me I had just barely crossed over into our own country; the last 150 yards of my glide had landed me clear of the Germans.

The soldiers also said we had better try to move the machine, as the Germans could see it from the hill opposite and would be sure to shell it in a very little while.

With the help of several other men from a field artillery battery we hauled the machine into a little valley just before the German shells began to arrive. One dropped with a noisy bang some 200 yards away from us, and I fell flat on my stomach. I hadn't seen much land fighting up to this time, but I had been told that that was the proper thing to do. The Tommies, however, looked at me with amazement. The idea of anybody dropping for a shell 200 yards away! They told me there was nothing to worry about for the moment, and added, cheerfully, that in a few minutes the Huns would be doing a little better shooting.

But I had my own back with the Tommies sooner than I could ever have hoped for. This time a shell landed about twenty yards from us, and down went everybody but me. I stood up—out of sheer ignorance! I didn't know by the sound of the shell how close it was going to land, but the others did and acted accordingly. The joke of the whole thing was that the shell was a "dud." It didn't explode, and I had the laugh on the wise artillerymen.

Eventually we got the machine behind a clump of trees where the Germans couldn't see it, and they decided to waste no more ammunition hunting us out. Although it was already 6 o'clock in the evening, I started to work on the engine, but after an hour and a half had not succeeded in getting a single cough out of any one of the many cylinders. So I decided to let matters rest and accept a very cordial invitation to spend the night with a battery near by.

It would have been a very interesting night indeed if I could have had some real place to sleep, or if I had not been wearing loose, heavy flying-clothes, with fleece-lined boots up to my hips, or if it had not commenced to rain about 9 o'clock, or if in the middle of the night a heavy artillery battle had not started. But in spite of the discomfort and the drizzle it was all very interesting and exciting, and seemed to me a sort of fitting sequel to my wonderful first day of combat in the air.

The next day it continued to rain, and as I received no word from my squadron in answer to several telegrams, I borrowed some tools from the gunners and again got to work on my choked-up engines. Within a few hours she was running beautifully. Now the problem was to find a place from which to fly off. The ground was rough and very muddy, but I decided to try to "taxi" over it. We had not bumped very far along, however, the machine and I, when a big piece of mud flew up and split the propeller. That ended it. There was nothing to do but wait for help to come from the squadron. It came the next afternoon, after I had spent a terrible night trying to get to the squadron, and rescue parties from the squadron had spent an equally terrible night trying to get to me. I had landed at a point which had been well behind the German lines a few days ago, where the roads had been mined and blocked in all manner of ways, and where the German spirit of wanton destruction had held high carnival. I had even tried to get through in a Ford, but it was no use.

It was about 3 o'clock the second afternoon after I

landed that one of the rescue parties arrived. They had travelled about 90 miles to get to me, although the aerodrome was only 15 miles away. By the third afternoon we had succeeded in taking my machine to pieces, and having safely loaded it into a motor lorry, began our return journey about 7 o'clock in the evening. We arrived at the aerodrome at 6.30 the next morning. I slept part of the way, but never was so worn out and tired in all my life, for many times during the night it was necessary to get out and help our car out of the mud. Finally, when about six miles from the aerodrome, we went into a mudhole and stuck. It was absolutely impossible to move in any direction, so with one of the men I set out on foot to an aerodrome about three miles away. There I pulled some sleepy mechanics out of bed and got them to drive me to my own aerodrome a little farther along.

Now for the first time I learned exactly what had happened in the fight on the 25th. The patrol leader had also destroyed one of the enemy machines, while the third Hun had escaped. All of us were perfectly safe and none of our machines damaged except my own, which showed a few tears from shell fragments.

It seemed to me it had been ages since the fight. But at last I was back among my companions—and I had the large total of one machine to my credit. There were fellows in the squadron who did not have any, however, and I was very proud—so proud and excited over the whole episode that, despite my intense weariness, I couldn't go to sleep until late in the afternoon.

CHAPTER 5

THE FATES had been so kind to me in my first fight in the air, that the next time I crossed the lines my squadron commander had designated me as patrol leader. I knew this was a difficult job, but it was not until after we started out that I knew *how* difficult. First of all, I seemed to be leading too fast; then the pace would become too slow. Some of the machines seemed too close to me, and some too far away. I wondered why it was that everyone should be flying so badly to-day except myself. As a matter of fact, if I had been leading properly, the other machines would have found it quite easy to keep in their assigned places.

However, one learns by experience, so at the end of two hours I was leading much better, and had progressed another step in the school of war-flying. The clouds were very thick this day and rolled under us at times in great cumulus masses. We caught only occasional glimpses of the ground through rifts in the clouds a mile or more apart. It was necessary to watch very closely through these holes and to recognize familiar places on the ground, otherwise we were likely to get lost and never see home again. When our two hours' tour of duty aloft was ended, though, we landed safely at the aerodrome without having seen any enemy machines.

Two days later my patrol engaged in one of the bitterest

57

fights I have ever known. I knew that night the full meaning of that last line so often seen in the British official communiqué: "One of our machines did not return." A second machine barely reached our lines, with the pilot so badly wounded he lived but a little while.

The patrol consisted of a flight of six machines. I led my companions up to 12,000 feet before heading across the trenches just south of Arras. Once over the lines, we turned to the north, not penetrating very far into Hunland because of the strong wind that was blowing about fifty miles an hour from the west. These westerly gales were one of the worst things we had to contend with at the front. They made it very easy for us to dash into enemy territory, but it was a very different story when we started for home and had to combat the tempest. If an airman ever wishes for a favouring wind, it is when he is streaking for home.

Seeing the modern war-aeroplanes riding through howling storms reminds one that it was not so long ago that a ten-mile breeze would upset all flying-plans for a day at any aerodrome or exhibition field. Now nothing short of a hurricane can keep the machines on the ground. As far as the ability to make good weather of it is concerned, the airman of to-day can laugh at a gale and fairly take a nap sitting on a forty-mile wind.

We had been over the lines twenty minutes, and were tossing about a bit in the storm, when I sighted an enemy machine flying about half a mile below me. He was scudding gracefully along just over the top of a layer of filmy white clouds. I signalled to the remainder of my patrol that I had sighted an enemy, and in another instant I was diving after him. As I sped downward I could see the remainder of the patrol coming after me. I must have been plunging fully 150 miles an hour at the German with the black crosses on his wings, when suddenly out of the clouds, and seemingly right under my nose, a second enemy machine appeared. I realized now that we were in for serious fighting, that we had run into an ambuscade, for it was a great trick of the Germans at this time to lurk behind patches of clouds to obtain the advantage of a surprise attack. We soon taught them, however, that this was a game at which two could play.

When the second machine loomed so suddenly from his hiding-place, I naturally transferred my attention to him. I closed to within 150 yards and then opened fire from directly behind. Nothing happened, however, for all my bullets seemed to be going far wide of their mark. I was frankly surprised at this and wondered what had happened to the marksmanship which had stood me in such good stead in my first fight. As a result of these thoughts I neglected to look behind me to see if the other machines of the patrol were following, and my first intimation that anything was wrong was the sound of machine guns firing from somewhere in the rear. I was about to turn my head to see if it was one of the patrol firing, when some flaming German bullets shot past between my left-hand planes. Then I realized that a third enemy machine had arrived on my tail and had a dead shot at me. There was but one way to get out of this, and I tried it. I pulled my machine right up into the air and turned over backward in a partial loop. As I did so the enemy machine flashed by underneath.

It was a narrow escape, but it gave me a breathing-spell in which to look around for the remainder of my patrol. They were nowhere to be seen. Later I learned that when they were coming down to me, more enemy machines had popped out of the clouds, and there had been a sort of general mêlée. The machine which got on my tail seemed to have dropped out of the clear sky above. In all, it turned out, there were about ten of the enemy to six of us.

It was my luck to be mixed up single-handed with three of the Huns. Under the circumstances, wisdom seemed to me the better part of valour, and I climbed as speedily as I could, eventually managing to get clear of their range. Then, looking around, I saw a fight going on about a mile farther east. It was a matter of thirty seconds to fly into this, and there I found two of my machines in a go at four or five of the enemy. We fought for fifteen minutes or more without either side gaining an advantage. During all this time, however, we were steadily being driven by the gale farther and farther into German territory, and were rapidly losing height as well. We estimated at this time we must be fully fifteen miles behind the Hun lines.

We had circled and dived and fought our way down to about 4000 feet when suddenly about half a mile away I saw one of our patrol fighting for his life with two of the enemy. I broke off the futile engagement we were in and flew to the lone pilot's assistance. The other two of my pilots also broke away from the Germans and followed me as I headed over to help him. At the same moment he succeeded in escaping from the two attacking Huns, and we joined up again in a formation of four machines.

At this time we were as low as 2500 feet, but by careful flying and using the clouds to hide in, we managed to evade all the enemy flyers who came swirling after us.

The moment we headed for home, however, all the "Archies" in the neighbourhood opened fire on us. We were flying straight into the teeth of the fifty-mile gale and were making very little headway against it. This slow pace made us an easy mark for the guns, and meant that we had to do a lot of dodging. We darted from one cloud to another, using them as much as possible for protection. It was again the old instinct of "taking cover" or "digging in."

Reaching the aerodrome, we were very much crestfallen. The battle had not been a success, and two of our patrol, two of our most intimate friends, had not returned. Later that night, about 11 o'clock, we had word that one of the missing machines had landed on our side of the lines with the pilot badly wounded. Next morning we heard the particulars of a wonderful piece of work done by this gallant boy. He was only eighteen, and had been in France but three weeks. The British Flying Corps is filled with boys of that age—with spirits of daring beyond all compare, and courage so self-effacing to be a continual inspiration to their older brothers in the service.

In the early part of the fight this boy had been hit by an explosive bullet, which, entering him from behind, had pierced his stomach and exploded there. His machine had been pretty badly shot about, the engine damaged, and, therefore, a great resulting loss in efficiency. Mortally wounded as he was, however, he fought for ten or fifteen minutes with his opponents and then succeeded in escap-

61

ing. Dazed from pain and loss of blood, he flew vaguely in a westerly direction. He had no idea where he was, but when the anti-aircraft guns ceased to fire, he glided down and landed in a field. Stepping out of his machine, he attempted to walk, but had moved scarcely forty steps when he fell in a faint. He was hurried to hospital and given the tenderest of care, but next morning he died, leaving behind a brave record for his brief career in the flying service.

The pilot who did not return was reported missing for about two months, and then we heard he had been killed outright, shot dead in the air. Upon looking back on this fight now, in the light of my later experience, I wonder that any of us got out of it alive. Every circumstance was against us, and the formation we ran into was made up of the best Hun pilots then in the air. They fought under as favourable conditions as they could have wished, and one can only wonder how they missed completely wiping us out.

Next day there were only four of us left in my patrol, but we were assigned to escort and protect six other machines that were going over to get photographs of some German positions about ten miles behind the front-line trenches. I had my patrol flying about a thousand feet above the photography machines when I saw six enemy single-seater scouts climbing to swoop down upon our photography machines. At the same time there were two other enemy machines coming from above to engage us.

Diving toward the photography machines, I managed to frighten off two of the Boches; then, looking back, I saw one of my pilots being attacked by one of the two higher Germans who had made for us. This boy, who is now a prisoner of war, had been a school-mate of mine before the war. Forgetting everything else, I turned back to his assistance. The Hun who was after him did not see me coming. I did not fire until I had approached within 100 yards. Then I let go. The Hun was evidently surprised. He turned and saw me, but it was too late now. I was on his tail—just above and a little behind him—and at fifty yards I fired a second burst of twenty rounds. This time I saw the bullets going home. As was the case with the first machine I brought down, this one also flopped over on its back, then got into a spin, and went headlong to the earth, where it crashed a hopeless wreck.

I rejoined the photography machines, which unfortunately in the meantime had lost one of their number. We brought the five home safely, and the photographs were a huge success.

CHAPTER 6

It was a German boast at this time that their retreat from the Somme had upset the offensive plans of the British and French for months to come. How untrue this was they were soon to know. We Canadians knew that the first big "push" of the spring was to come at Vimy Ridge, where the Canadian Corps had been holding the line grimly the entire winter through. It had been a trying ordeal for our men, who were almost at the foot of the ridge with the Germans everywhere above them.

During all the long cold months of winter the old Boche had been looking down on us, pelting the infantry in the trenches with all manner of bombs and trench-mortar shells, and making life generally uncomfortable. During all this time, however, and in spite of the fact that the Germans had direct observation both of our lines and the country behind them, we had succeeded in massing a hitherto unheard-of number of guns and great forces of reserves for the initial attack of the new fighting season.

About April 1st we heard the first rumours of the approaching storm. The British artillery was tuning up all along the line, the greatest fire being concentrated in the neighbourhood of Arras and the Vimy Ridge, running north from that quaint old cathedral city. It was the beginning of that great tumult of artillery which eventually was to practically blow the top off the ridge—and the Germans with it. Our machines had been operating with the guns, ranging them on the German lines and the villages where the enemy troops were quartered in the rear. There had been much careful "registering" also of the German battery positions, so that when the time came for our troops to "go over," the British and Canadian artillery could pour such a torrent of shells on the German guns as to keep them safely silent during the infantry attack.

At last came the orders for our part in another phase of the "show." It was up to us to "clear the air" during the last days of battle preparation. We did not want any more prying eyes looking down upon us from the clouds— it was bad enough to have to submit to the ground-observation from the German-held ridges. We were already accustomed to fighting the enemy aeroplanes over their own ground and thus keeping them as far as possible from our lines, but now we were assigned to a new job. It was attacking the enemy observation balloons. They flew in the same places almost every day—well back of the enemy lines; but the observers in them, equipped with splendid telescopes, could leisurely look far into our lines and note everything that was going on. We proposed to put out these enemy eyes.

We called the big, elongated gasbags "sausages" and the French did likewise—"saucisses." They floated in the air at anywhere from 800 to 3000 feet above the ground, and were held captive by cables. These cables were attached to some special kind of windlasses which could pull the balloons down in an incredibly short space of time. Sometimes they would disappear as if by witchcraft. Wherever the sausages flew they were protected from aeroplane attack by heavy batteries of anti-aircraft guns, and also by what we came to know as "flaming onions." These "flaming onions" appear to consist of about ten balls of fire, and are shot from some kind of rocket gun. You can see them coming all the way from the ground, and they travel just too fast to make it possible to dodge them. I have never had an "onion" nearer than 200 feet from me, but the effect of these balls of fire reaching for you is most terrifying, especially the first time you have the pleasure of making their acquaintance.

Our instructions were not only to drive the enemy balloons down, but to set fire to and destroy them. This is done by diving on them from above and firing some incendiary missile at them—not by dropping bombs on them, as one so often hears in London.

The British attack at Arras and Vimy was set for April 9th—Easter Monday. On April 5th we started after the sausages. The weather at this time was very changeable, chilling snow-squalls being intermingled with flashes of brilliant warm sunshine. It was cloudy and misty the day our balloon attacks began, and the sausages were not visible from our side of the lines. I was assigned to "do in" a particularly annoying sausage that used to fly persistently in the same place day after day. It was one of the sausages with a queer-shaped head, looking for all the world like a real flying pig—sans feet. Any new sort of hunting always appealed to me strongly, and I was eager for the chase when I crossed into enemy territory in search of my particular game. I flew expectantly in the direction where the balloon usually inhabited the air, but it was nowhere to be seen. I circled down close to the ground to be sure it was not on duty, and immediately found myself in the midst of a terrific fire from all manner of guns. Something told me to hurry away from there, and I did. The quickest shelter available was a rather dark and forbidding cloud, but I made for it with all my might, climbing as fast as my little single-seater would take me. What a relief it was to be lost in that friendly mist. Continuing to climb, I rose at last into the sunshine and then headed for home. My balloon had not been up, but my first experience as a sausage hunter had not been the pleasantest form of amusement, and I was inclined not to like it very much. Later on I met with some success against the balloons; but the sport, while exciting, was not to be compared with another aeroplane.

The weather cleared late in the afternoon of the 5th, and for the first time in my flying career I had the privilege of going out alone in search of a fight. There was not an enemy machine in the air, however, and I returned with nothing to report.

Next morning, bright and early, I was again out "on my own" in search of adventure. I had been flying over the lines for over half an hour when suddenly I spied an enemy machine about a mile over in Hunland, and some distance above me. In these days I no longer had any misgivings as to whether a machine was friend or foe—I had learned to sense the enemy. Our greatest difficulty at the time was drawing the Huns into a close combat. I set out to see what sort of fighting material this particular pilot of the Iron Crosses was made of. Keeping him always within view, I climbed to nearly 15,000 feet, and from that point of vantage dived upon him. I waited until my plunge had carried me to within 150 yards of him before opening fire. I had given him a burst of probably twenty rounds, when my gun jammed. The Hun saw me and dived away as fast as he could go. I dived after him, tinkering with the gun all the time, and, finally getting it clear, fired another burst at 100 yards. This drove him into a still deeper dive, but he flattened out again, and this time I gave him a burst at 50 yards. His machine evidently was damaged by my fire, for he now dived vertically toward the ground, keeping control, however, and landing safely in a field.

This fight gave me a new resolve—to devote more time to target practise. I should have destroyed this Hun, but poor shooting had enabled him to escape. Going home, I spent an hour that day practising at a square target on the ground. Thereafter I gave as much time as possible to shooting practise, and to the accuracy I acquired in this way I feel I owe most of my successes. Aeroplane target practise is not without its dangers. The target on the ground is just about the size of the vital spots you aim at in fighting. You have to dive steeply at this, and there is a very little margin of safety when plunging at full speed to within a few feet of the earth.

April 6th and 7th were memorable days in the Flying Corps. The public, knowing nothing of the approaching attack which was to go down in history as the Battle of Arras, was distinctly shocked when the British communiqués for these two days frankly admitted the loss of twenty-eight of our machines. We considered this a small price to pay for the amount of work accomplished and the number of machines engaged, coupled with the fact that all of our work was done within the German lines. In the two days that we lost twenty-eight machines, we had accounted for fifteen Germans, who were actually seen to crash, and thirty-one driven down damaged, many of which must have met a similar fate. The British do not officially announce a hostile machine destroyed without strict verification. When you are fighting a formation of twenty or more Huns in a general mêlée, and one begins a downward spin, there is seldom time to disengage yourself and watch the machine complete its fatal plunge. You may be morally certain the Hun was entirely out of control and nothing could save him, but unless someone saw the crash, credit is given only for a machine driven down. The Royal Air Force is absolutely unperturbed when its losses on any one day exceed those of the enemy, for we philosophically regard this as the penalty necessarily entailed by our acting always on the offensive in the air.

Technically, the Germans seldom gave a machine "missing," for the fighting is practically always over their territory, and every one of their machines driven down can be accounted for, even if it is totally destroyed. Many of our losses are due wholly to the fact that we have to "carry on" over German territory. Any slight accident or injury that compels a descent in Hunland naturally means the total loss of the British machine. But such a loss does not involve a German victory in combat; it is merely a misfortune for us. If the machine could only have reached our side of the lines it might have been repaired in half an hour. The public often forgets these things when reading of British machines that fail to return.

Every class of our machines was now engaged in the preparations for the big offensive. The bombing squadrons were out by day and by night. They would fly over the lines with only the stars to guide them and drop tons of high-explosive wherever it was considered that the resulting damage would have a crippling effect upon the defensive power of the German machine. Our photographers were busy during every hour of sunlight, and our artillery observing machines were keeping long hours in company with the guns, carrying on the preliminary bombardments.

My own experiences on April 7th brought me my first decoration—the Military Cross. The thrills were all condensed into a period of two minutes for me. In that time I was fortunate enough to shoot down an enemy machine and destroy the "sausage" I had started for two days before. This should have been excitement enough, but I added to it by coming within 15 feet of being taken a German prisoner and becoming an unwilling guest of the Huns—for the "duration."

I was ordered after my particular balloon and had climbed to about 5000 feet before heading for the lines. On my way there I had to pass over one of our own observation-balloons. I don't know what it was that attracted my attention, but, looking down, I saw what appeared to be two men descending in parachutes. A moment later the balloon below me burst into flames. I saw the enemy machine which had set it on fire engaged with some of ours, but as I had definite orders to proceed straight to the lines and destroy the hostile balloon which had been allotted to me, I was unable to join in the fighting.

Just about this time an amusing incident was in progress

at our aerodrome. A Colonel of the Corps was telephoning my squadron commander, informing him that one of our balloons had just been destroyed.

"Well, if it is any consolation, young Bishop, of my squadron, has just gone over to get one of theirs," replied my commander.

"Good God," said the Colonel, "I hope he has not made a mistake in balloon and set ours on fire!"

At this moment I was serenely sailing over the enemy trenches, keeping a sharp lookout for some sign of my own balloon. After flying five miles over the lines, I discovered it and circled around as a preliminary to diving down upon it. But just then I heard the rattle of machine guns directly behind me and saw bullet-holes appear as if by magic in the wings of my machine. I pulled back as if to loop, sending the nose of my machine straight up into the air. As I did so the enemy scout shot by underneath me. I stood on my tail for a moment or two, then let the machine drop back, put her nose down, and dived after the Hun, opening fire straight behind him at very close range. He continued to dive away with increasing speed, and later was reported to have crashed just under where the combat had taken place. This victory I put down entirely to luck. The man flew directly in line with my gun and it would have been impossible to have missed him.

I proceeded now to dive for the balloon, but having had so much warning, it had been pulled down to the ground. I would have been justified in going home when I saw this, for our orders were not to go under 1000 feet after the sausages. But I was just a bit peevish with this particular balloon, and to a certain extent my blood was up. So I decided to attack the ungainly monster in its "bed." I dived straight for it and when about 500 feet from the ground, opened fire. Nothing happened. So I continued to dive and fire rapid bursts until I was only 50 feet above the bag. Still there were no signs of it catching fire. I then turned my machine gun on the balloon crew, who were working frantically on the ground. They scattered and ran all about the field. Meantime a "flaming onion" battery was attempting to pelt me with those unsavoury missiles, so I whirled upon them with a burst of twenty rounds or more. One of the onions had flared within a hundred yards of me.

This was all very exciting, but suddenly, with a feeling of faintness, I realized that my engine had failed. I thought that again, as during my first fight, the engine had oiled up from the steep diving I had done. It seemed but a moment before that I was coming down at a speed that must have been nearly 200 miles an hour. But I had lost it all in turning my machine upon the people on the ground.

There was no doubt in my mind this time as to just where I was, and there appeared no alternative but to land and give myself up. Underneath me was a large open field with a single tree in it. I glided down, intending to strike the tree with one wing just at the moment of landing, thus damaging the machine so it would be of little use to the Huns, without injuring myself.

I was within 15 feet of the ground, absolutely sick at heart with the uselessness of it all, my thoughts having turned to home and the worry they would all feel when I was reported in the list of the missing, when, without warning, one of my nine cylinders gave a kick. Then a second one miraculously came to life, and in another moment the old engine—the best old engine in all the world—had picked up with a roar on all the nine cylinders. Once again the whole world changed for me. In less time than it takes to tell it, I was tearing away for home at a hundred miles an hour. My greatest safety from attack now lay in keeping close to the ground, and this I did. The "Archies" cannot fire when you are so close to earth, and few pilots would have risked a dive at me at the altitude which I maintained. The machine guns on the ground rattled rather spitefully several times, but worried me not at all. I had had my narrow squeak for this day, and nothing could stop me now. I even had time to glance back over my shoulder, and there, to my great joy, I saw a cloud of smoke and flames rising from my erstwhile *bête noir*—the sausage. We afterward learned it was completely destroyed.

It was a strange thing to be skimming along just above the ground in enemy territory. From time to time I would come on groups of Huns who would attempt to fire on me with rifles and pistols, but I would dart at them and they would immediately scatter and run for cover. I flew so low that when I would come to a clump of trees I would have to pull my nose straight up toward the sky and "zoom" over them. Most of the Germans were so startled to see me right in their midst, as it were, they either forgot to fire or fired so badly as to insure my absolute safety. Crossing the three lines of German trenches was not so comfortable, but by zigzagging and quick dodging I negotiated them safely and climbed away to our aerodrome. There I found that no bullets had passed very close to me, although my wing-tips were fairly perforated.

That evening I was delighted to get congratulations not

only from my Colonel, but from my Brigadier as well, supplemented later by a telegram from the General Commanding the Flying Corps. This I proudly sent home the same evening in a letter.

CHAPTER 7

EASTER SUNDAY was one of the most beautiful days I have ever seen, and we felt that at last the gods of the weather were going to smile on a British offensive. The sky was a wonderful blue, flecked only here and there with bits of floating white clouds. There was a warmth of spring in the sunshine that filled one with the joy of living. Hundreds of our machines were aloft to demonstrate anew the fact that we were masters of the air. They carried the fighting wholly into the enemy's territory, sought out his aerodromes, his military headquarters, his ammunition dumps, his concentration camps, and challenged him in every possible manner to come up and fight. Some of our reconnaissance machines flew from sixty to ninety miles behind the German lines.

It used to amuse and amaze me to think, on days like this, of the marvels that modern flying had accomplished. Our machines were not only called upon to fly faster by far than the swiftest birds, but to do "stunts" that no bird ever thought of. Whoever heard of a bird flying upside-down? Yet there were plenty of our pilots who rather delighted in doing this. There are trick flyers just as there are trick bicyclists and trick riders in the circus. I belonged to the steady flyers' class, but some day soon I am really going to learn to fly, to do aerial acrobatics, and everything. I remember crossing the lines one day in the hottest sort of "Archie" fire and suddenly seeing below me one of the most remarkable sights of my flying-career. The shape of the machine looked a little familiar, and the colour was certainly familiar. But there was something queer about the rigging. My curiosity was aroused, and in spite of the whistling "Archie" shells I determined to have a closer look at this stranger of the air. As I approached I made out something that looked like wheels stuck up toward the sky. I was more puzzled than ever for a moment, then realized it was a machine upside-down. The wing-tips bore the red, white, and blue target markings of the British service, so I flew very close to see if anything was wrong. When I got near enough I recognized my squadron commander at the time. He was out having an afternoon stroll and had deliberately sailed over the lines upside-down, just to show his contempt for the Hun "Archies," and also in the hope that he might attract the attention of a "head-hunter," and thus bring on a little excitement.

With the great attack scheduled for dawn the next morning, we went at our work on Easter Sunday with an added zest. At 9 o'clock, just after the early-morning mist had been driven away by the mounting sun, I was due for an offensive patrol—in other words, there were six of us going over the lines in search of trouble. Our squadron commander was in the flight, and he had been leading us inside Hunland for about twenty minutes before anything happened. Then a two-seated machine, with the enemy markings on it, appeared underneath us. Our commander dived at him like a hawk, and his first burst of fire clearly hit home. The enemy machine dived toward the ground, but thinking this might be a trick I dived after it, firing all

78

the way. I soon saw, however, that the Huns actually had been hurt and were doomed. So I pulled my machine out of the dive and looked around for the rest of the patrol. They had all disappeared. A moment or two later I sighted a pair of our machines engaged in a helter-skelter fight to the left of me, and had just started in their direction, when, seemingly out of nowhere at all, an enemy scout dived at me. I turned quickly and avoided him. Then for several minutes we had a running fight, firing occasionally, but neither one of us being able to manœuvre into a position of real advantage. Finally, the enemy flew away eastward and escaped.

In the excitement of the fighting I had not noticed it before, but now, looking downward, I saw a Boche sausage just beneath me. I plunged at it just as the crew began to pull it frantically down. I kept diving and firing at the big bag, but as no smoke appeared I gathered I had either missed it all the while, or my bullets had failed in their duty as "fire-bugs."

I had dropped to 800 feet in my chase after the bag and could plainly see German troops marching toward the support and reserve lines at the front. Evidently they were preparing for our assault. The way our artillery had been going for a week past left them little room for doubt. I flew about watching these troops for some time, despite the tell-tale rattle of the machine guns on the ground, but at last decided I had better get out of it. I saw a cloud some distance above me and decided to climb into it and lose myself. I had just about reached the edge of the cloud when another enemy scout decided to have a go at me. I had fired about a hundred rounds at him when my gun jammed.

79

I dodged away to have time to correct this, and the enemy, immediately seeing his advantage, dived after me. He was using explosive bullets, and I could see them burst near me from time to time. One hit the machine about 3 feet from where I was sitting and exploded, but did no material damage. A little more dodging from these ungentlemanly missiles, and a little more work, and my gun was right again. So I turned upon my pursuer. We fought round and round each other for a seemingly interminable time, when at last I saw my chance, darted behind him and gave him a short burst of fire. No effect. A second later I got him within my sights again, and this time I fired very carefully. His machine gave a shiver, then began tumbling toward the earth completely out of control. I followed to within a few hundred feet of the ground, and as it was still plunging helplessly, I turned away.

The sky around me now seemed entirely deserted. It gave me time to speculate as to whether I should climb up to a nice, safe height of about two miles and then fly home, or whether I should streak it across the trenches as I had done the day before. Recalling some incidents of yesterday's adventures, however, I decided to climb! I proceeded upward in wide sweeping circles, looking all the time for any trace of my missing comrades. They were not visible, even at 10,000 feet, so I flew around a bit more in the hope of finding them.

My search was rewarded, not by meeting my friends, but by the sudden appearance of two Hun machines flying in the direction of our lines. Drawing a little to one side so as to have a good look at them, I discovered they were being escorted and protected by three other machines flying well back of and above them. By quick thinking I estimated I could make a running attack on the lower two before the upper three could get into the affair. I closed in and fired a burst at the nearer of the two, but the second one got on my tail and, firing very accurately, gave me some of the most uncomfortable moments of my fighting-career. One of his bullets grazed my cap as it passed my head, then crashed through the little wind-screen just in front of me. This was too much, so, leaving my pursuit of the first machine, I turned and paid attention to Number 2. Hun Number 1, in the meantime, evidently decided he had had enough, for he kept flying away as fast as he could. In turning on the second machine I chanced to find myself in an ideal position, and my first burst of fire sent him spinning in an uncontrolled nose-dive, which ended a few seconds later in a "crash" just beneath me.

I figured that by this time the upper three were due, and, turning, found all of them diving for me, firing with all their guns. There was no time for any choice of tactics on my part, so I headed for the enemy machines and flew directly under them, managing to get in a good burst of fire upward at the leading two-seater that seemed particularly anxious for a fight. He wasn't as anxious as I had thought, for after the first exchange of shots he kept diving away and did not return. The other two, however, remained on the "field" of battle. I estimated by this time that I had only about forty rounds of ammunition left for my gun; but again there was no real choice for me. I had either to fight or be attacked in a very nasty position; so I fought. My two adversaries had seen the previous combats, and when I showed fight toward them they seemed none too anxious to prolong the fray. I had just finished my last bullet when the two of them dived away in opposite directions and left me —"lord of all I surveyed."

There was not another machine in the sky now, and, thankful for that fact, I headed for home with my throttle pushed wide open, and landed without any more excitement. When I handed in my report, especially the part dealing with the fight with the formation of five enemy machines, some of the squadron looked on me as some sort of wild man or fire-eater just escaped from the Zoo. The Colonel telephoned up and said that I had better not fly any more that day, so I was given the afternoon off.

As we had to be ready to fly with the dawn next morning, we were early to bed on Easter night. As we turned in, the British guns were roaring all along the far-reaching battle-line. The whole horizon was lighted with their flashes, like the play of heat-lightning on a sultry summer evening. I knew the meaning and the menace in the booming of the cannon, but I slept the sound slumber of a little child.

CHAPTER 8

DAWN WAS DUE at 5.30 o'clock on Easter Monday, and that was the exact hour set for the beginning of the Battle of Arras. We were up and had our machines out of the hangars while it was still night. The beautiful weather of a few hours before had vanished. A strong, chill wind was blowing from the east and dark, menacing clouds were scudding along low overhead.

We were detailed to fly at a low altitude over the advancing infantry, firing into the enemy trenches, and dispersing any groups of men or working troops we happened to see in the vicinity of the lines. Some phases of this work are known as "contact patrols," the machines keeping track always of the infantry advance, watching points where they may be held up, and returning from time to time to report just how the battle is going. Working with the infantry in a big attack is a most exciting experience. It means flying close to the ground and constantly passing through our own shells as well as those of the enemy.

The shell fire this morning was simply indescribable. The bombardment which had been going on all night gradually died down about 5 o'clock, and the Germans must have felt that the British had finished their nightly "strafing," were tired out and going to bed. For a time almost complete silence reigned over the battlefields. All along the German lines star-shells and rocket-lights were looping through the darkness. The old Boche is always suspicious and likes to have the country around him lit up as much as possible so he can see what the enemy is about.

The wind kept growing stiffer and stiffer and there was a distinct feel of rain in the air. Precisely at the moment that all the British guns roared out their first salvo of the battle, the skies opened and the rain fell in torrents. Gunfire may or may not have anything to do with rainmaking, but there was a strange coincidence between the shock of battle and the commencement of the downpour this morning. It was beastly luck, and we felt it keenly. But we carried on.

The storm had delayed the coming of day by several minutes, but as soon as there was light enough to make our presence worth while we were in the air and braving the untoward elements just as the troops were below us. Lashed by the gale, the wind cut our faces as we moved against the enemy. The ground seemed to be one mass of bursting shells. Farther back, where the guns were firing, the hot flames flashing from thousands of muzzles gave the impression of a long ribbon of incandescent light. The air seemed shaken and literally full of shells on their missions of death and destruction. Over and over again one felt a sudden jerk under a wing-tip, and the machine would heave quickly. This meant a shell had passed within a few feet of you. As the battle went on the work grew more terrifying, because reports came in that several of our machines had been hit by shells in flight and brought down. There was small wonder of this. The British barrage fire that morning was the most intense the war had ever known. There was a greater concentration of guns than at any time during the Somme. In fact, some of the German prisoners said afterward that the Somme seemed a Paradise compared to the bombardments we carried out at Arras. While the British fire was at its height the Germans set up a counter-barrage. This was not so intense, but every shell added to the shrieking chorus that filled the stormy air made the lot of the flying man just so much more difficult. Yet the risk was one we could not avoid; we had to endure it with the best spirit possible.

The waves of attacking infantry as they came out of their trenches and trudged forward behind the curtain of shells laid down by the artillery were an amazing sight. The men seemed to wander across No Man's Land, and into the enemy trenches, as if the battle was a great bore to them. From the air it looked as though they did not realize that they were at war and were taking it all entirely too quietly. That is the way with clock-work warfare. These troops had been drilled to move forward at a given pace. They had been timed over and over again in marching a certain distance, and from this timing the "creeping" or rolling barrage which moved in front of them had been mathematically worked out. And the battle, so calmly entered into, was one of the tensest, bitterest of the entire world-war.

For days the battle continued, and it was hard work and no play for everybody concerned. The weather, instead of getting better, as spring weather should, gradually got worse. It was cold, windy, and wet. Every two or three hours sudden snowstorms would shut in, and flying in these squalls, which obliterated the landscape, was very ticklish business.

On the fourth day of the battle I happened to be flying about 500 feet above the trenches an hour after dawn. It had snowed during the night and the ground was covered with a new layer of white several inches thick. No marks of the battle of the day before were to be seen; the only blemishes in the snow mantle were the marks of shells which had fallen during the last hour. No Man's Land itself, so often a filthy litter, was this morning quite clean and white.

Suddenly over the top of our parapets a thin line of infantry crawled up and commenced to stroll casually toward the enemy. To me it seemed that they must soon wake up and run; that they were altogether too slow; that they could not realize the great danger they were in. Here and there a shell would burst as the line advanced or halted for a moment. Three or four men near the burst would topple over like so many tin soldiers. Two or three other men would then come running up to the spot from the rear with a stretcher, pick up the wounded and the dying, and slowly walk back with them. I could not get the idea out of my head that it was just a game they were playing at; it all seemed so unreal. Nor could I believe that the little brown figures moving about below me were really men—men going to the glory of victory or the glory of death. I could not make myself realize the full truth or meaning of it all. It seemed that I was in an entirely different world, looking down from another sphere on this strange, uncanny puppet-show.

Suddenly I heard the deadly rattle of a nest of machine guns under me, and saw that the line of our troops at one place was growing very thin, with many figures sprawling on the ground. For three or four minutes I could not make out the concealed position of the German gunners. Our men had halted, and were lying on the ground, evidently as much puzzled as I was. Then in a corner of a German trench I saw a group of about five men operating two machine guns. They were slightly to the flank of our line, and evidently had been doing a great amount of damage. The sight of these men thoroughly woke me up to the reality of the whole scene beneath me. I dived vertically at them with a burst of rapid fire. The smoking bullets from my gun flashed into the ground, and it was an easy matter to get an accurate aim on the German automatics, one of which turned its muzzle toward me.

But in a fraction of a second I had reached a height of only 30 feet above the Huns, so low I could make out every detail of their frightened faces. With hate in my heart I fired every bullet I could into the group as I swept over it, then turned my machine away. A few minutes later I had the satisfaction of seeing our line again advancing, and before the time had come for me to return from my patrol, our men had occupied all the German positions they had set out to take. It was a wonderful sight and a wonderful experience. Although it had been so difficult to realize that men were dying and being maimed for life beneath me, I felt that at last I had seen something of that dogged determination that has carried British arms so far.

The next ten days were filled with incident. The enemy fighting machines would not come close to the lines, and there was very little doing in the way of aerial combats, especially as far as I was concerned, for I was devoting practically all of my time to flying low and helping the

87

infantry. All of our pilots and observers were doing splendid work. Everywhere we were covering the forward movement of the infantry, keeping the troops advised of any enemy movements, and enabling the British artillery to shell every area where it appeared concentrations were taking place. Scores of counter-attacks were broken up before the Germans had fairly launched them. Our machines were everywhere behind the enemy lines. It was easy to tell when the Germans were massing for a counter-stroke. First of all our machines would fly low over the grey-clad troops, pouring machine-gun bullets into them or dropping high-explosive bombs in their midst. Then the exact location of the mobilization point would be signalled to the artillery, so that the moment the Germans moved our guns were on them. In General Orders commending the troops for their part in the battle, Field-Marshal Sir Douglas Haig declared that the work of the Flying Corps, "under the most difficult conditions," called for the highest praise.

We were acting, you might say, as air policemen. Occasionally one of our machines would be set upon by the German gangsters—they were "careful" fighters and seldom attacked unless at odds of four to one—and naturally we suffered some casualties, just as the ordinary police force suffers casualties when it is doing patrol duty in an outlaw country. The weather was always favourable to the German methods of avoiding "open-air" combats. Even the clearer days were marked by skies filled with clouds sufficiently large and dense enough to offer protection and hiding-places to the high winging Hun machines.

I had several skirmishes, but did not succeed in bringing down another machine until April 20th, when I was fortunate enough to begin another series of extremely interesting and successful fights. I was promoted to be a Captain about this time and thought I was very happy; but the promotion was followed by another incident which really made me proud. The sergeants of my squadron had made me a round "nose" for my machine. It fitted on the propeller head and revolved with it. I had it painted a brilliant blue, and from that time on my machine was known as "Blue Nose." It was given to me, the Sergeant-Major explained, as a sign that I was an "Ace"—that I had brought down more than five machines. I was so pleased with this tribute from the men that I took old "Blue Nose" visiting to several other squadrons, where I exhibited my new mark of distinction to many of my friends and flying companions.

The machine I got on April 20th was the first I ever destroyed in flames. It is a thing that often happens, and while I have no desire to make myself appear as a blood-thirsty person, I must say that to see an enemy going down in flames is a source of great satisfaction. You know his destruction is absolutely certain. The moment you see the fire break out you know that nothing in the world can save the man, or men, in the doomed aeroplane. You know there is no "camouflage" in this, and you have no fear that the enemy is trying any kind of flying trick in the hope that he will be left alone.

I was flying over a layer of white clouds when I saw a two-seater just above me. We generally met the enemy in force during these days, but this German machine was all alone. Neither the pilot nor observer saw me. They flew along blissfully ignorant of my existence, while I carefully kept directly underneath them, climbing all the time. I was only ten yards behind the Hun when I fired directly up at him. It had been an exciting game getting into position underneath him, carefully following every move he made, waiting, hoping, and praying that he would not see me before I got into the place I wanted. I was afraid that if he did see me I would be at a distinct disadvantage below him. My hand must have been shaky, or my eye slightly out, because, although I managed to fire ten rounds, I did not hit anything vital. Even in this crucial moment the humour of the situation almost got the better of me. My machine seemed so little, carefully flying there under the big, peaceful Hun, who thought he was so safe and so far from any danger. Suddenly, from just underneath him, he heard the "tat-tat-tat-tatter-tatter" of my machine gun almost in his ear, the range was so close. Then he must have seen my smoking bullets passing all around him. Anyway, there was consternation in the camp. He turned quickly, and a regular battle in the air began between the two of us. We manœuvred every way possible, diving, rolling, stalling; he attempting to get a straight shot at me, while my one object was to get straight behind him again, or directly in front of him, so as to have a direct line of fire right into him.

Twice I dived at him and opened fire from almost point-blank range, being within two lengths of him before I touched the lever which set my gun to spouting. But there was no success. The third time I tried a new manœuvre. I dived at him from the side, firing as I came. My new tactics gave the German observer a direct shot at me from his swivel gun, and he was firing very well too, his bullets passing quite close for a moment or two. Then, however, they began to fly well beyond my wing-tips, and on seeing this I knew that his nerve was shaken. I could now see my own bullets hitting the right part of the Hun machine, and felt confident the battle soon would be over.

I pulled my machine out of its dive just in time to pass about 5 feet over the enemy. I could see the observer evidently had been hit and had stopped firing. Otherwise the Hun machine seemed perfectly all right. But just after I passed I looked back over my shoulder and saw it burst into flames. A second later it fell a burning mass, leaving a long trail of smoke behind as it disappeared through the clouds. I thought for a moment of the fate of the wounded observer and the hooded pilot into whose faces I had just been looking—but it was fair hunting, and I flew away with great contentment in my heart.

This fight seemed to have changed my luck for the better. Everywhere I went for the next few weeks enemy machines were easily found, and I had numerous combats, many of them successful. Some days I could have been accused of violating all the rules of a flying men's union (if we had had one). I would fly as much as seven and a half hours between sunrise and sunset. Far from affecting my nerves, the more I flew the more I wanted to fly, the better I seemed to feel, and each combat became more and more enjoyable. Ambition was born in my breast, and, although I still dared not entertain hope of equalling the record of the renowned Captain Ball, who by this time had shot down over thirty-five machines, I did have vague hopes of running second to him.

Along with the new ambition there was born in me as well a distinct dislike for all two-seated German flying machines! They always seemed so placid and sort of contented with themselves. I picked a fight with the two-seaters wherever I could find one, and I searched for them high and low. Many people think of the two-seater as a superior fighting machine because of its greater gun-power. But to me they always seemed fair prey and an easy target. One afternoon, soon after this new Hun hatred had become a part of my soul, I met a two-seater about three miles over the German lines and dived at him from a very low height. As bad luck would have it, my gun had a stoppage, and while I turned away to right it, the enemy escaped. Much disgusted, I headed away homeward, when into my delighted vision there came the familiar outlines of another Hun with two men aboard. I flew at this new enemy with great determination; but after a short battle he dived away from me, and although I did my best to catch him up, I could not. He landed in a field underneath me. To see him calmly alight there under perfect control filled me with a towering rage. I saw red things before my eyes. I vowed an eternal vendetta against all the Hun two-seaters in the world, and, the impulse suddenly seizing me, I dived right down to within a few feet of the ground, firing a stream of bullets into the machine where it was sitting. I had the satisfaction of knowing that the pilot and observer must have been hit, or nearly scared to death, for, although I hovered about for quite a long time, neither of them stepped from the silent machine.

Half an hour after this occurrence I saw one of our machines in difficulties with three of the enemy. The Huns were so engrossed with the thought that they had a single British machine at their mercy, I felt there was a good chance that I might slip up and surprise them. My scheme worked beautifully. I came up to within 15 yards of one of the Huns, and, aiming my machine at him with dead accuracy, shot him down with my first ten bullets. He probably never knew where the bullets came from, not having the slightest idea another British machine was any-where in that part of the sky. I turned now to assist with the other two Huns, but by this time my brother-pilot had sent one of them spinning out of control, while the last remaining enemy was making good his escape as fast as his Mercédès engine could pull him through the air. It is surprising sometimes how much dead resistance there is in the air when you are in a hurry. Having nothing better to do under the circumstances, I dived down after my own victim to get a view of the crash. I was just in time. He struck the ground at the corner of a field, and what was one instant a falling machine was next a twisted bit of wreckage.

CHAPTER 9

IT WAS APPARENT to us by this time that the Germans were bringing their best pilots opposite the British front to meet the determined offensive we had been carrying on since April 1st. Most of the machines we met were handled in a manner far above the German average. Each night our pilots brought in exciting stories of the chase. Although they were a higher class of fighting men than we had hitherto flown against, the Germans still showed a reluctance to attack unless they outnumbered us by at least three to one. One lone German was induced to take a fatal chance against a British scout formation. By clever manœuvring, at which the hostile airman was also quite adept, we managed to entice him to attack one of our machines from behind. As he did so, a second British machine dived at him, and down he went, one of his wings breaking off as he fell.

I can best illustrate the German tactics of the time by telling the experience of one of our faithful old photographic machines, which, by the way, are not without their desperate moments and their deeds of heroism. All of which goes to show that the fighting scouts should not get all the credit for the wonders of modern warfare in the air. The old "photographer" in question was returning over the lines one day when it was set upon by no less than eleven hostile scouts. Nearly all the controls of the

95

British machine were shot away, and the observer, seriously wounded, fell half-way out of the nacelle. Although still manœuvring his machine so as to escape the direct fire of the enemies on his tail, the British pilot grasped the wounded observer, held him safely in the machine, and made a safe landing in our lines. A moment later the riddled aeroplane burst into flames. Under heavy shell-fire the pilot carried the wounded observer to safety.

One of the distinguished German flying squadrons opposite us was under command of the famous Captain Baron von Richthofen. One day I had the distinction of engaging in three fights in half an hour with pilots from this squadron. Their machines were painted a brilliant scarlet from nose to tail—immense red birds, they were, with the graceful wings of their type, Albatross scouts. They were all single-seaters, and were flown by pilots of undeniable skill. There was quite a little spirit of sportsmanship in this squadron, too. The red German machines had two machine guns in fixed positions firing straight ahead, both being operated from the same control.

The first of my three fights with these newcomers in our midst occurred when I suddenly found myself mixed up with two of them. Evidently they were not very anxious for a fight at the moment, for, after a few minutes of manœuvring, both broke it off and dived away. Ten minutes later I encountered one of the red machines flying alone. I challenged him, but he wouldn't stay at all. On the contrary, he made off as fast as he could go. On my return from chasing him I met a second pair of red Huns. I had picked up company with another British machine, and the two Huns, seeing us, dived into a cloud to escape.

I went in after them, and on coming out again found one directly beneath me. On to him I dived, not pulling the trigger until I was 15 yards away. Once, twice, three times I pressed the lever, but not a shot from my gun! I slipped away into another cloud and examined the faithless weapon, only to find that I had run completely out of ammunition. I returned home quite the most disgusted person in the entire British Army.

During the changeable days of the Arras offensive we had many exciting adventures with the weather. On one occasion I had gone back to the aircraft depot to bring to the front a new machine. Sunshine and snow-squalls were chasing each other in a seemingly endless procession. On the ground the wind was howling along at about fifty miles an hour. I arrived at the depot at 9 o'clock in the morning, but waited about until four in the afternoon before the weather appeared to be settling down to something like a safe and sane basis. The sunshine intervals were growing longer and the snow periods shorter, so I climbed into my machine and started off. It was only a fifteen minutes' fly to the aerodrome, but in that time a huge black cloud loomed up and came racing toward me. I was headed straight into the gale, and the way was so rough from the rush of the wind and the heavy clouds floating by that the little machine was tossed about like a piece of paper. Several times I thought I was going to be blown completely over. Occasionally, without any warning, I would be lifted a sheer hundred feet in the air. Then later I would be dropped that distance, and often more. I was perspiring freely, although it was a very cold day. It was a race against the weather to reach my destination in time.

One cannot see in a snowstorm, and I felt that if the fleecy squall struck me before I sighted the aerodrome I would have to land in a ploughed field, and to do this in such a gale would be a very ticklish proposition. Added to all this, I was flying a machine of a type I had never handled before, and naturally it was a bit strange to me. Nearer and nearer the big cloud came. But I was racing for home at top speed. About half a mile from the haven I sought, the storm struck me. The moment before the snow deluge came, however, I had recognized the road that led to the aerodrome, and coming down to 50 feet, where I could just make it out, I flew wildly on, praying all the time that the snow striking my engine would not cause it to stop. Then the awful thought came to me that perhaps I was on the wrong road. Then, even more suddenly than it had come, the snow stopped—the storm had swept right over me. There, just ahead of me, I saw the tents and hangars and the flying pennant of the aerodrome—home. This was my first experience in flying through snow, and I did not care for another.

A few days after my unsuccessful experience with the red Richthofen scouts, I got my just revenge and a little more back from the Huns. My Major had been told to have some photographs taken of a certain point behind the German lines, and by special permission he was given the privilege of taking them himself. The point to be photographed was about seven miles in German territory, and in order to make a success of the snapshotting it would be necessary to have a strong escort. The Major offered to go out and do the photographs on his own without an escort, but the Colonel would not hear of it, and so it was arranged that an offensive patrol would go out at 9 o'clock in the morning, meet the Major at a given point, and escort him over the ground he wished to cover.

My patrol was the one working at the time, and I was the leader. At 9.30 we were to meet, just east of Arras, at 6000 feet. The rendezvous came off like clockwork. I brought the patrol to the spot at 9.28, and two minutes later we spied a single Nieuport coming toward us. I fired a red signal light and the Nieuport answered. It was the Major. I then climbed slightly and led the patrol along about 1000 feet above the Nieuport in order to protect the Major and at the same time keep high enough to avoid too much danger from anti-aircraft fire. We got to the area to be photographed without any other excitement than a very heavy greeting from the "Archies." There were a number of big white clouds floating around about 6000 feet, and these made it difficult for the guns to shoot at us. But they also made it difficult for the Major to get his photographs. We went around and around in circles for what seemed an eternity. During one of these sweeping turns I suddenly saw four enemy scouts climbing between two clouds and some distance off. I knew they would see us soon, so it occurred to me it would be a brilliant idea to let the enemy think there was only one British machine on the job. Under these circumstances I knew they would be sure to attack, and then the rest of us could swoop down and surprise them. I had no intention of letting the Major in for any unnecessary risks, but it seemed such a rare chance, I could not resist it.

I led the patrol about 2000 feet higher up and there we waited. The enemy scouts did not see us at all, but they did see the Major. And they made for him. The first the Major knew of their approach, however, was when they were about 200 yards away, and one of them, somewhat prematurely, opened fire. His thoughts—he told me afterward—immediately flew to the patrol, and he glanced over his shoulder to see where we were. But we had vanished. He then wondered how much money he had in his pockets, as he did not doubt that the four Huns, surprising him as they had, would surely get him. Despite these gloomy and somewhat mercenary thoughts, the Major was fighting for his life. First he turned the nose of his machine directly toward the enemy, poured a burst of bullets toward a German at his right; then turned to the left, as the second machine approached in that direction, and let him have a taste of British gunfire as well. This frightened the first two Huns off for a moment, and, in that time, I arrived down on the scene with the rest of the patrol.

One of the Huns was firing at the Major's machine as I flashed by him, and I fired at a bare ten yards' range. Then I passed on to the second enemy machine, firing all the while, and eventually passing within 5 feet of one of his wing-tips. Turning my machine as quickly as I could, I was yet too late to catch the other two of the formation of four. They had both dived away and escaped. I had hit the two that first attacked the Major, however, and they were at the moment falling completely out of control 1000 or more feet below me, and finally went through the clouds, floundering helplessly in the air.

This little interruption ended, we all reassembled in our

former positions and went on with the photographing. This was finished in about fifteen minutes, and, under a very heavy anti-aircraft fire, we returned home. The episode of the four Huns was perhaps the most successful bit of trapping I have ever seen, but it was many weeks before the squadron got through teasing me for using our commander as a decoy. I apologized to the Major, who agreed with me that the chance was too good a one to miss.

"Don't mind me," he said; "carry on."

CHAPTER 10

JUST TO SHOW there was no ill-feeling, the Major that afternoon proposed some excitement of an entirely different sort. There was no patrol marked down for us, so the Major took another pilot and myself out on a sort of Cook's tour. We called it "seeing the war." We all piled into an automobile, drove through poor old shell-torn Arras, which was fairly stiff with troops moving up toward the front and with relieved divisions that were coming out of the line for hard-earned rest. Occasionally there was the screech of a "Whistling Percy" overhead—a shell from a long-range 16-inch naval gun some miles beyond the German lines. It was vastly different from flying, this motoring through Arras, threading your way tediously in and out of the marching troops and the interminable traffic of offensive warfare.

Finally, we passed the railway-station, which had long been a favourite target for the German gunners, but still showed some semblance of its former utility; turned "Dead Man's Corner" into the road for Cambrai, proceeded over what had once been our front line, then over the old No Man's Land, and finally came to a halt some miles beyond the city. There we left the car behind the crest of a hill, and out of direct observation from the enemy trenches, which were not very far away. We were very bold, we three musketeers of the upper air, as we set out on foot, without a guide, to make our way toward a German machine that had been brought down a few days before just inside our lines.

On the way we had to pass about thirty batteries of artillery, and as no one said anything to us we presumed we were all right in strolling along in front of them. The guns seemed harmless enough, sitting there so cold and silent. However, before we had gone so very far, a man crawled out of a hole in the ground and told us that if we were going anywhere in particular we had better hurry, as a battle was due to start in just five minutes. We questioned him about the "show," and then decided to walk on as fast as we could and reach the village of Monchy, which sat a mass of ruins on a little hill, and was just 200 yards within our lines.

Monchy-le-Preux, to give the little town the full dignity of its Artois name, is about five miles east of Arras, and was the final fixed objective of the Easter drive. It is the highest bit of ground between Arras and the German border. Around it swirled some of the most desperate fighting of the entire war. It had been a pretty little place up to a few days before, but the moment the Germans had been driven from their defensive works about the village, many of them at the point of the bayonet, the German artillery was turned on Monchy in a perfect torrent of explosive shells. What had once been houses quickly disappeared, or were dissolved into jagged ruins. Our infantry had found three bed-ridden French civilians still living in Monchy when we took it, but fortunately for them they had been passed back to one of our hospitals before the Boche started his destructive bombardments.

It was just 3 o'clock when all the guns behind us opened fire over our heads. I must admit that I was at least "nervous" for the next half-hour. Shells were going over us by the thousand, and pretty soon the Germans started their retaliatory fire. Many of the Boche shells landed quite near to us. We could see them explode and throw up from the ground great fountains of earth and débris, but we could not hear them on account of the roar of our own artillery.

There we were, the three of us, in the midst of a battle that we didn't know a thing on earth about. My nervousness grew perceptibly as I looked around and realized that in the whole of the country there was not another soul walking about. Everyone was under cover, or dug in somewhere, except us three. However, we decided there was no going back; so we went on.

Our taking refuge in Monchy was surely a case of ignorance being bliss. We crawled into the wrecked village, having passed, without knowing it, another "Dead Man's Corner" far deadlier than the one in Arras itself. This Monchy corner had a speciality of its own—machine-gun fire. The Germans used to rake it many times a day. Evidently they were engaged in some other nefarious occupation as we walked blithely by the place, on into the village, then down the main street, picking our way carefully in a zigzag course among the débris. About this time another good Samaritan hailed us. He came dashing out of a house and told us to run for cover. Not knowing any cover of our own, we followed him to his. He led us into a deep dugout the Germans had built during their occupation of the town. We told our guide and friend that we wanted to move on very shortly, but he laughed and said we would have no choice in the matter for the next few hours. He knew the habits of the Huns in that particular locality. Promptly at 4 o'clock the Germans began their daily bombardment. Our friend and guide, now turned philosopher, told us the Germans had the dugout "registered" very accurately, and it would be unsafe to move from it until the firing was over for the day. We were shut up in this hole for an hour or more, when we decided to take our chances and go home.

We were very much worried, in the meantime, that our car, resting on the high-road, might have been hit. Everything pointed to the fact that it was time for us to go. So, in a temporary lull, we crawled out and made a dash through the village. We did not leave by the same way we had come. We knew too much by this time of "Dead Man's Corner." Once clear of Monchy we noticed that a large number of shells were dropping in a sort of barrier about 400 yards in front of us. We pressed on, nevertheless, in the hope that there would be a sufficient lull in the firing to let us slip through the shell line. No lull appeared imminent, however, so we turned away to the right to avoid the particular spots that apparently had aroused the Germans' ire. We had not gone far when a huge shell dropped about 30 yards from us. It knocked two of us clean off our feet and on our backs in the mud. It was rude, we thought, to treat three unoffending airmen out for a holiday like this, so we were more than ever anxious to get out of it all. At last we arrived at some derelict tanks, left over from last week's battles, and there we found an ammunition column passing back from the guns. We climbed aboard one of the empty limbers, glad of the lift, and gladder still of the company of these imperturbable khaki soldiers who were taking the events of the afternoon with that strange spirit of boredom one so often finds up near the firing-lines.

We told the drivers we had left our car over the hill near a stranded tank, and they assured us they were going in that very direction. So we sat peacefully on the rattling limber for a mile or more. Then, being quite certain we were going the wrong way, we inquired of the ammunition-column men how far it was to their tank. They said it was just ahead of us. We looked. There was a tank, quite all right, but it was not *our* tank. A little more explaining to the soldiers that were now quite plentiful about us, and we were informed that our tank was at least a mile and a half away. We had made a stupid mistake, but we paid for it in the muddy walk we had back.

The car was perfectly safe when we got to it, and some time later we returned to the aerodrome right as rain. We had picked up a lot of souvenirs during our walk into Monchy and out again, and felt like Cook's tourists indeed when Tommies on the way would look at us with a tolerant smile.

These were wonderfully interesting days to me. Late the next afternoon I had the good fortune to be a spectator of the greatest fight in the air I have ever seen. Thrilling fights are often witnessed from the ground, but more of them take place at heights so misty that ground observers know nothing of them, unless one or more of the combatants should come tumbling down in a crash. More than often fights in the air would go unobserved if it were not

107

for the "Archie" shells breaking in the sky. These shells play about friend and foe alike, but when you are really intent upon an air duel the "Archies" make no impression upon you whatever.

It was my privilege this day to see the spectacular fight from my machine. I had been idling along in the afternoon breeze, flying all alone, when I saw in the distance a great number of machines, whirling, spinning, and rolling in a great aerial mêlée. I made toward them as fast as I could go, and as I approached watched the fight carefully. It was very hard to tell for a time which machines were ours and which were the Huns'. Coming nearer it was easier, for then the Huns could be distinguished by the brilliant colouring of many of their machines.

Hunting the Huns had taken on a new interest at this time because suddenly their machines had appeared painted in the most grotesque fashion. It was as if they had suddenly got an idea from the old Chinese custom of painting and adorning warriors so as to frighten the enemy. We learned afterward that it was just a case of the spring fancies of the German airmen running riot with livid colour-effects. We wanted to paint our machines, too, but our budding notions were frowned upon by the higher officers of the Corps. But every day our pilots were bringing home fresh stories of the fantastic German creations they had encountered in the skies. Some of them were real harlequins of the air, outrivalling the gayest feathered birds that had winged their way north with the spring. The scarlet machines of Baron von Richthofen's crack squadron, sometimes called the "circus," heralded the new order of things. Then it was noticed that some of the enemy craft were painted with great rings about their bodies. Later, nothing was too gaudy for the Huns. There were machines with green planes and yellow noses; silver planes with gold noses; khaki-coloured bodies with greenish-grey planes; red bodies with green wings; light blue bodies and red wings; every combination the Teutonic brain could conjure up. One of the most fantastic we had met had a scarlet body, a brown tail, reddish-brown planes, the enemy markings being white crosses on a bright green background. Some people thought the Germans had taken on these strange hues as a bit of spring camouflage; but they were just as visible or even more so in the startling colours they wore, and we put it down simply to the individual fancies of the enemy pilots.

The battle seemed to be at about evens, when suddenly I saw a German machine, brightly coloured, fall out of the mêlée, turning over and over like a dead leaf falling from a tree late in autumn. I watched it closely for what seemed an awful length of time, but finally it crashed a complete wreck. Turning my eyes to the fight again, I saw one of our own machines fall out of control. Half-way between the scrimmage and the ground I thought it was coming into control again, but it turned into another dive and crashed near the fallen Hun. A moment later a second German machine came tumbling out of the fight. Eaten up with anxiety to get into the fight myself, I could not help having a feeling akin to awe as I watched the thrilling struggle. A mass of about twelve machines was moving around and around in a perfect whirlwind, and as I approached I could see our smoking bullets and the flaming missiles of the Huns darting in all directions.

Just as I reached the scene, the fight, unfortunately for me, broke up, and my participation in it was limited to a short chase and a few shots after the fleeing Germans.

Balloon attacks now came into fashion again, and for a short time we were told to attack them every day. In my case most of these attacks were unsuccessful. One day I crossed after a balloon only 2000 feet up. Although I flew as fast as I could to reach the "sausage," it had been hauled down before I got to it. Despite this, I flew low and attacked the gasbag, but with no apparent results. The balloon still sat there peacefully on the ground. Some enemy machines were in the distance attacking one of the men of my squadron who was after another "sausage," and I flew to his assistance and managed to frighten them off. I then returned to the balloon, had another go at it—but again no result. It was discouraging work.

That day, out of three of us who crossed to attack the balloons, one man was lost. His experience was rather a bitter one, but he fought death under such a heavy handicap and with such bravery that his story is worthy of relation as one of the traditions of the Royal Flying Service. It was his first attack on the balloons, and he crossed the lines with me. We separated when about half a mile over. When he dived after his balloons, two Hun machines got on his tail, and with their first burst of fire managed to hit both of his legs, breaking one. A second afterward a shot went through his petrol tank, and the inflammable liquid poured over his helpless legs. But, wounded as he was, he fought back at the Germans and managed to get back over our lines. The two Germans, realizing he was badly hit, kept after him, and with another burst of fire shot away all his controls and at the same time set fire to the machine. It dived to the earth a flaming torch, and crashed. Some brave Tommies who were near rushed frantically into the blazing wreckage, and pulled the unfortunate pilot out. He was taken to a hospital, where we found him, badly burned, one leg and one arm broken, and several bullet wounds in his body.

For two weeks he improved steadily, and we all had high hopes of his recovery. Then the doctors found it necessary to amputate his broken leg, and two days later the poor lad died. He had been in France but a few weeks.

"I came half-way round the world from Australia to fight the Hun," he told one of our men in hospital. "I served through the campaign at Gallipoli as a Tommy, and at last I got where I longed to be—in the Flying Corps. It seems hard to have it end like this so soon."

There was joy in flying these later days in April when a tardy spring at last was beginning to assert itself. The hardness of the winter was passing and the earth at times was glorious to see. I remember one afternoon in particular when the whole world seemed beautiful. We were doing a patrol at two miles up about 6 o'clock. Underneath us a great battle was raging, and we could see it all in crisp clearness, several lines of white smoke telling just where our barrage shells were bursting. The ground all about the trenches and the battle-area was dark brown, where it had been churned up by the never-ceasing fire of the opposing artillery. On either side of the battle-zone could be seen the fields, the setting sun shining on them with

111

the softest of tinted lights. Still farther back—on both sides—was the cultivated land. The little farms stood out in varying geometric designs, with different colours of soil and shades of green, according to what had been sown in them and the state of the coming crops. There was no mist at all, and one could see for miles and miles.

From Arras I could see the Channel, and it resembled more a river of liquid gold than a sea. Across the Channel it was possible to make out England and the Isle of Wight. The chalk cliffs of Dover formed a white frame for one side of the splendid picture. Toward Germany one could see a tremendous wooded country, a stretch of watered lowlands beyond the trees, and the rest indistinct. To the south I could make out a bit of the River Seine, while to the north lay the Belgian coast. The marvellous beauty of it all made the war seem impossible. We flew peacefully along for miles in the full enjoyment of it all, and I shall always be glad we did not have a fight that evening. It would have brought me back to stern reality with too sudden a jerk.

A few days later I was away from the beauties in life and after the grossly hideous balloons again. Success rewarded one of my earnest efforts. It happened one morning when we had been patrolling the air just above the trenches. It was a very dull morning, the clouds being under 3000 feet. Well across the lines I could make out the portly form of a German balloon sitting just under them. The sight of the "sausage" filled me with one of those hot bursts of rage I had so often in these days against everything German in the world. After the finish of the patrol, I had my machine filled up with petrol, and, with a good supply of special ammunition, started out on a voluntary expedition to bring down that fat and self-satisfied balloon. Upon nearing the lines I flew up into the clouds, having taken a careful compass bearing in the exact direction of my intended victim. Flying slowly at a rate of sixty miles an hour, I crept steadily forward, taking reckonings now and then from the compass and my other flying-instruments. I figured the balloon was six miles over the lines, and as I had climbed into the clouds about one mile behind our own lines, I reckoned that seven minutes should let me down just where I wanted to be. I popped out of the clouds with every nerve tense, expecting to find the "sausage" just beneath me. Instead, I found nothing, not even a familiar landmark. I felt pretty sick at heart when I realized I had lost myself. My compass must have been slightly out of bearing, or I had flown very badly. At the moment I had no idea where I was. I flew in a small circle, and then spied another balloon quite near me. The balloon had seen me first, the "S.O.S." had gone out, and it was being hauled down with miraculous swiftness. I dived for the descending German as hard as I could go, and managed to get within 50 yards while it was still 800 feet up. Opening fire, I skimmed just over the top of the balloon, then turned to attack again, when, to my great joy, I saw the bag was smoking. I had seen no one leap from the observer's basket hanging underneath, so I fired a short burst into it just to liven up anybody who happened to be sitting there. The "sausage" was then smoking heavily, so I flew south in the hope of finding some landmark that would tell me the way home.

Suddenly another balloon loomed before me, and at the

same time I recognized by the ground that it was the "sausage" I had first set out to attack. I fired the remainder of my ammunition at it at long range, but had no effect so far as I could see. I then came down to 15 feet of the ground and flew along a river-bank that I knew would lead me home. I had found this low flying over enemy-land quite exhilarating, and rather liked the sights I used to see.

During the next week I had three or four very unsatisfactory combats. My work consisted mostly of sitting patiently over the lines, waiting for an enemy to appear. Then, after it had put in an appearance, I would carefully watch for an opportunity and attack, only to have the Hun escape. I was mostly concerned with my old friends the enemy two-seaters, especially the ones that would fly at low altitudes doing artillery observation work. I would try to get behind a cloud, or in one, and surprise them as they went by. I managed to pounce upon several machines from ambush, but had no luck at all in the succeeding combats. On such occasions I would return much disgusted to the aerodrome and put in more time at the target.

I began to feel that my list of victims was not climbing as steadily as I would have liked. Captain Ball was back from a winter rest in England and was adding constantly to his already big score. I felt I had to keep going if I was to be second to him. So I was over the enemy lines from six to seven hours every day, praying for some easy victims to appear. I had had some pretty hard fighting. Now I wanted to shoot a "rabbit" or two. Several times while sitting over the lines I was caught badly by anti-aircraft fire, and had to do a lot of dodging and turning

114

to avoid being badly hit by the singing shrapnel shells. As it was, I frequently returned with scars, where bits of shell had pierced my planes and fuselage.

One day I saw a two-seater flying calmly along about three miles high. I started to climb up under him, and it seemed to me I was hours on the way, for he had seen me and was climbing as well. Eventually I reached his level, but we were then nearly four miles from the earth. The air was so thin I found it difficult to get my breath. It was coming in quick gasps and my heart was racing like mad. It is very difficult to fly a single-seater at such altitudes, much more to fight in one. The air is so rare that the small machines, with their minimum of plane surface, have very little to rest upon. The propeller will not "bite" into the thin atmosphere with very much of a pull. But despite all this, I decided to have a go at the big German two-seater, and we did a series of lazy manœuvres. I realized I was unable to put much energy into the fighting, and the only shot I got at the Hun I missed! At the height we had met, the Hun machine was faster than mine, so in a few minutes he broke off the combat and escaped.

I spent half an hour under another enemy machine, trying to stalk him, but he finally got away. During the time I was "hiding" under the two-seater I was quite happy in the belief that he could not bring a gun to bear on me. But when I landed I found several bullet-holes in the machine close to my body. After that I kept a sharper lookout on the fellows upstairs.

One day, after climbing slowly to 17,000 feet and still finding no victims, I flew fifteen miles inside the German lines, hoping to catch some unwary enemy aloft. At last,

115

about half a mile beneath me, I saw a lone scout. I carefully manœuvred to get between him and the sun, for once there I knew he could not see me and I would have all the advantage of a surprise attack. I was within 20 yards, and going about 130 miles an hour, when I opened fire. Not more than ten shots had sped from my gun when the Hun went spinning down in a nose-dive, seemingly out of control. I dived after him, firing steadily, and we had dropped something like 3000 feet when the enemy machine burst into flames.

During my dive I had seen a black speck in the distance which looked as if it might be a Hun. So I climbed again and made in the direction of the speck, hoping it would turn out to be an enemy machine. It did, and I succeeded in getting in another surprise attack, but my shots hit no vital spot and the German slid away in safety.

A few minutes later I saw a third Hun, and again I manœuvred for the advantage of the sun position. But the pilot either saw me before I got into the blinding rays, or else he saw the other machine diving away and thought something was wrong, for he, too, dived steeply before I could get within effective range.

However, I was very well pleased with the day's work, for I had sent my second machine down in flames. Such an incident has never failed to put me in a good humour. It is so certain and such a satisfactory way of destroying Huns.

CHAPTER 11

APRIL 30TH was a red-letter day for me. I celebrated it by having a record number of fights in a given space of time. In one hour and forty-five minutes I had nine separate scraps. This was during the morning. Before we had tea that afternoon, the Major and I had a set-to with four scarlet German scouts that was the most hair-raising encounter I have ever been mixed up in.

This very pleasant fighting-day started when I led my patrol over the lines, and dived so steeply after an enemy machine which suddenly appeared beneath me that I nearly turned over. The remainder of the patrol lost me completely. I kept putting the nose of my Nieuport down until I got beyond the vertical point. I fell forward in my seat and struck my head against the little wind-screen. I was going down so fast I upset my aim completely, and allowed the Hun, by a quick manœuvre, to escape me altogether. The patrol had disappeared, so I climbed up as fast as I could to have a look around.

Five minutes later I saw two huge Huns directly over our lines. They were easily mammoths of the air. I wanted to have a look at the strangers, so started in their direction, keeping my own level, which was a little beneath the big Germans. They grew rapidly in size as I approached, and I took them to be some new type of two-seater. From later experiences and diagrams I have seen, I think now they must have been the three-seater Gothas—like the machines that later flew over London so often, many of them coming to grief as the penalty of their daring.

This was probably the first appearance of the Gothas over our lines. A few days later I had another glimpse of two of them in the distance; but that was the last I saw of the monstrous Germans. This day they seemed rather keen for a fight, and one of them came down in a slow spiral to get at me. I, at the same time, was trying to stay in the "blind spot" just beneath him, and hoped eventually to get a steady shot at some vital point. We must have made a ludicrous picture, little me under the huge Hun. I felt like a mosquito chasing a wasp, but was willing to take a chance.

While manœuvring with the first monster, the second one dived at me from a slight angle, and seemed to open fire with a whole battery of machine guns. I dived to gain a little more speed, then pulled my nose straight up into the air and opened fire. When I had got off about fifteen rounds, the gun jammed, and I had to dive quickly away to see what was wrong. I found I could do nothing with it in the air; but my aerodrome was only a few miles away, so I dived down to it, corrected the jam, and was away again in a few minutes in search of more excitement.

I was very peevish with myself for having missed a chance to bring down one of the big new German machines, and was in a real fighting temper as I recrossed the lines. I had not gone far on my way when I saw three of the enemy about two miles away, doing artillery work. I dived for the nearest one and opened fire. Then I had the somewhat stirring sensation of seeing flaming bullets coming from all three of the Huns at once in my direction. The odds were three to one against me, and each enemy machine had two guns to my one, but suddenly they quit firing, turned, and fled away. I went after them, but quickly saw the game they were attempting to play. They were trying to lead me directly under five scarlet Albatross scouts.

These scarlet machines, as I have explained before, all belonged to von Richthofen's squadron. I saw them just in time to turn away. I drew off about a mile, then easily outclimbed my brilliant red rivals. Having gained the advantage of position, I decided to have a go at the crack German flyers. I dived toward them with my gun rattling, but just before reaching their level I pulled the machine up and "zoomed" straight up in the air, ascending for a short distance with the speed of a rocket. Then I would turn and dive and open fire again, repeating the performance several times. The Huns evidently had expected me to dive right through them, but my tactics took them by surprise and they began to show nervousness. After the third "zoom" and dive, the formation broke up and scattered.

Then I turned around to look for the treacherous two-seaters who had sought to lead me into a veritable death-trap. I had searched several minutes before I picked them out of the sky, and I can still remember the thrill of joy with which I hailed them. It had seemed such a rotten trick, when they were three to one, not even to show fight, but simply try to trick me. I felt I must have vengeance, and went after them with the firm conviction that this time something was going to happen. I got into position where they would pass in front of me, and dived at the second Hun. His observer was firing at me, and pretty soon the other two Huns chimed in. Add to this staccato chorus the

119

healthy rattle of my own gun, and you may gain some idea of the din we were making in mid-air. My first twenty shots silenced the observer in the machine I was attacking, and as I passed over it, it suddenly slipped to one side, then stood on its nose, and fell. I did not have time to watch this machine down, but turned to attack the third Hun in the line. He had seen his comrade's fate, however, and, losing heart, had begun to dive away. I poured fifty rounds after him, then let him go. The leading machine had now disappeared, so I was left free to dive down and see what had happened to the Hun who had fallen out of the fight. He crashed in the most satisfactory manner. I turned and flew south, feeling very much better.

But I was not idle long. The five scarlet scouts had grouped together again and were approaching our lines farther south with the evident intention of attacking isolated British artillery machines. This particular squadron had made a habit of sneaking across our lines during the spring, and its leader had become known among our infantry as the "Little Red Devil," and one still hears him spoken of by the people who were in the trenches at that time. We had often tried to catch him on one of these expeditions, but he and his scarlet followers always chose a moment when our fighting patrols were engaged on another sector of the front. Then, dashing across the lines, the red Albatrosses would shoot down one of our older machines which we were employing then on observation work.

This morning I had an extra feeling of bitterness toward the Richthofens for their mean attempt to trick, and I went after them again with a feeling of exalted strength. I was above them as before, and, after one dive, they turned away east and gave up their idea of setting upon our artillery workers. I considered it unwise to go down and actually mix in the middle of them, as they were all good men. So I contented myself with harassing them from above, as I had done in the previous fight with the quintet that morning. They were apparently much annoyed at this, and kept steadily on their way east. I followed for quite a distance, and then sat over them as one by one they all went down and landed.

On the way home I had a skirmish with two German artillery machines, but we did not get within very close range of each other and nothing happened. They were frightened a bit, none the less, and sped away. In a little while, however, they plucked up courage and came back to resume their work of spotting for the German guns. This time I tried going at them from the front, and it proved exciting, to say the least. I approached the leading Hun of the pair head on, opening fire when about 200 yards away. He also opened fire about the same time. We drew nearer and nearer together, both firing as fast and direct as we could. I could see the Hun bullets going about 3 feet to one side of me, passing between my upper and lower planes. My own were doing better work, and several times it seemed certain that some of them were hitting the front of the enemy machine. On we came, each doing over a hundred miles an hour, which would have meant a collision impact of more than two hundred miles an hour. With big engines in front of us for protection, we were taking the risks of each other's bullets. Thirty yards away we were both holding to our course, and then, much to my relief, be it confessed, the Hun dived, and I thought I had

121

hit him. I turned quickly, but in doing so lost sight of him completely. Then a second later I saw him, some distance away, going down in a slight glide, evidently quite under control, but I think badly hit. The other machine followed him down and neither of them returned. I had very little ammunition left, but stayed on the lines another fifteen minutes hoping for one more fight.

It came when I sighted one of my favourites—an enemy two-seater—at work. I got directly above him, then dived vertically, reserving my fire until I was very close. The enemy observer had his gun trained up at me, and the bullets were streaming past as I came down. I missed him on my dive, so shot by his tail, then "zoomed" up underneath and opened fire from the "blind spot" there.

I don't know what was the matter with my shooting this morning, for, with the exception of the machine I bit from the side, it seemed to have become a habit with my enemies to dive away from me and escape. I did not seem to be able to knock them out of control. This one, like the others, dived steeply, and though I followed and fired all of my remaining bullets after him, he continued in his long straight dive and landed safely in the corner of a field near the city of Lens. Two or three "Archie" batteries took "bites" at me as I crossed the lines for luncheon.

Then came my thrilling adventure of the afternoon. The many experiences of the morning had put me in good humour for fighting, and immediately the mid-day meal was finished, I was up in the air again, with my squadron commander, to see if there were any Huns about looking for a bit of trouble. We patrolled along the lines for twenty minutes, but saw nothing in that time. Then, as I was leading, I headed further into enemy territory, and presently, to the south of us, we saw five Albatross scouts. We went after them, but before we had come within firing distance, we discovered four red Albatrosses just to our right. This latter quartette, I believe, was made up of Baron von Richthofen and three of his best men.

However, although we knew who they were, we had been searching for a fight, and were feeling rather bored with doing nothing, so after the four we went. The Major reached them first and opened fire on the rear machine from behind. Immediately the leader of the scouts did a lightning turn and came back at the Major, firing at him and passing within two or three feet of his machine. In my turn I opened fire on the Baron, and in another half-moment found myself in the midst of what seemed to be a stampede of bloodthirsty animals. Everywhere I turned smoking bullets were jumping at me, and although I got in two or three good bursts at the Baron's "red devil," I was rather bewildered for two or three minutes, as I could not see what was happening to the Major and was not at all certain as to what was going to happen to me.

It was a decided difference from the fighting of the morning. The Germans seemed to be out to avenge their losses, and certainly were in fighting trim. Around we went in cyclonic circles for several minutes, here a flash of the Hun machines, then a flash of silver as my squadron commander would whizz by. All the time I would be in the same mix-up myself, every now and then finding a red machine in front of me and getting in a round or two of quick shots. I was glad the Germans were scarlet and we were silver. There was no need to hesitate about firing when the right colour flitted by your nose. It was a lightning fight, and I have never been in anything just like it. Firing one moment, you would have to concentrate all your mind and muscle the next in doing a quick turn to avoid a collision. Once my gun jammed, and while manœuvring to the utmost of my ability to escape the direct fire of one of the ravenous Germans, I had to "fuss" with the weapon until I got it right again. I had just got going again when von Richthofen flashed by me and I let him have a short burst. As I did so, I saw up above me four more machines coming down to join in the fight. Being far inside the German lines, I at once decided they were additional Huns, so I "zoomed" up out of the fight to be free for a moment and have a look around. The moment I did this I saw the approaching machines were triplanes, belonging to one of our naval squadrons, and they were coming for all they were worth to help us against the Albatrosses. The latter, however, had had enough of the fight by now, and at the moment I "zoomed" they dived and flew away toward the earth. I did not know this until I looked down to where the fight should still have been in progress. There was nothing to be seen. Everybody had disappeared, including the Major. It was a sad moment for me, for I felt I had surely lost him this time. After circling over the spot for five minutes or more and exchanging signals with the triplanes, I started for home with a heavy heart.

On the way I saw another machine approaching me, and got into fighting position in the event it should prove hostile. As we drew nearer together I recognized it as another Nieuport, and then, to my great joy, I realized it was the Major. He had flown west at top speed as soon as he saw the fight was over and I was not to be seen. He was afraid I had followed the Huns down to the ground in my excitement, and was very anxious as to what had happened to me. Upon recognizing each other we waved our hands in the air, then came close enough together to exchange broad grins. We flew side by side to the aerodrome and landed. I found my machine had been very badly shot about, one group of seven bullets having passed within an inch of me in one place. It had been a close shave, but a wonderful, soul-stirring fight.

CHAPTER 12

THE FIRST FEW DAYS in May we spent escorting machines taking photographs. It was rather exciting work, for several times we went very long distances into Hunland and stayed over there for hours. It was also very nerve-racking work, as you listen constantly for the least break in the smooth running of your motor, knowing that if it fails you are too far from home ever to get there by gliding. At such times my thoughts always reverted to the ignominy one would feel in helplessly landing among the Germans and saying "Kamerad!" Far better to die in a fight, or even yield up the ghost to a despised "Archie," than tamely submit to being taken prisoner. Then, too, all the time you are loafing about taking snapshots from the air, the anti-aircraft fire gets very fierce.

On one occasion we went over to photograph an aerodrome in the vicinity of Douai, a city you can see from the top of Vimy Ridge on any clear day. We had with us in all about twenty machines, and were a very formidable party indeed. As luck would have it, we spied two Germans. With two or three other of our fighting pilots, I quickly dodged to one side to try to engage the Huns before they could see the whole crowd of us and be frightened away. But, no luck! They made off the minute we turned our noses in their direction. We proceeded over Douai, and in turning around once or twice, the machine actually taking the photographs was lost. I mean by lost that it got mixed up with the rest of us and it was practically impossible in that number of machines to pick it out again. The result was we went around and around in circles for half an hour trying to find out where it had gone. It was like an old-fashioned game of "Button, button, who's got the button?" and was so amusing I had to laugh. Around and around we went. The strain began to get on the nerves, of course, as every minute seemed to be an hour, and we all felt we should be getting away from there as soon as possible. But when you are in great danger, the smallest things make a keen appeal to your sense of humour, and the idea of the whole twenty of us playing such a foolish game in such a dangerous spot could not help having its funny side. Several of the others, on landing, told me they had felt the same way about it, and had had many good laughs.

Needless to say, the anti-aircraft guns under us were having the time of their unprincipled lives. They never had had such a huge bunch of good targets to shoot at, so they blazed into the midst of us with all the "hate" they had. But we had the luck, and hardly a machine was touched. We were flying at 13,000 feet, and that seemed lucky in itself. Many shells broke with loud bangs just under us and over us, but none at 13,000 feet. We were annoyed but not worried.

Finally, somebody got fed up with all this running around in aerial circles, and started toward home. We had all been waiting for something like that to happen, and every one of us streaked off in the leader's wake. We got back safely enough, but, to add to the fiasco of the expedition, it turned out that the man who was taking the photographs made some awful error and snapped the wrong places altogether. For a period of fully half an hour he had to listen patiently and quietly while the rest of us tried to think up a punishment to fit the crime. Later that afternoon we had to eat all our words, for while we were lunching and discussing the morning's work, the photographer pilot, all alone and without further orders, had quietly gone over the lines, taken the proper pictures, and returned safely with them. It was a brave thing to do, and we admired him for it.

The next day was a very successful one for me. I had several fights, and for one was later awarded the "Distinguished Service Order"—my second decoration. We had been taking photographs again, with another large escort, as on the day before, and were returning homeward when an enemy single-seater approached slightly below us. I went down and attacked him, and we fought for quite a while, exchanging shots now and then, with no result other than the escape of the enemy. The other machines had continued on their way and were nowhere to be seen when I climbed away from my unsuccessful duel. Being left alone, and of no further use to the photographers, I felt I might as well look around a bit. My search for enemy machines soon was rewarded. I came upon five of them doing artillery observation work. They were all two-seaters, and consequently my legitimate prey. The Huns were nicely arranged in two parties, one of two and the other of three. I decided that as the party of three was nearer, I would tackle it first. Remembering my former experience in diving into three enemy artillery machines, I was wary of a trap, but went after the bunch with a firm determination

I would not make a "hash" of it. The trio made away as I approached. Furious at the thought that they should escape scot-free, I forgot my caution and went after them pell-mell. I didn't care at the time whether there were any hostile fighting machines above me or not. I wanted to teach the cowardly two-seaters a justly deserved lesson. Catching up to within 200 yards of the rear one, I saw that all three were firing at me from their back guns. I was so much faster than the Huns I could zigzag on my course— wondering as I did so if I resembled an ocean greyhound dodging a submarine! Finally, I closed to within 20 yards of the fleeing Germans and let go at them. The rear machine was my easiest target. Soon I saw my bullets going into the observer's body and I feel sure some of them must have passed on from him to the pilot who was seated directly in front. The observer's face was white as a sheet, and, out of pure terror, I think, he had ceased to fire at me. The pilot now was gazing back over his shoulder and was too frightened to manœuvre his machine. He had turned into a sort of human rabbit, and was concerned only with running for his life. Fifteen rounds from my gun sufficed for that machine. Down it tumbled, a stricken and dying thing.

As the other two machines were some distance off. I did a circle to see the falling Hun crash. When I did this, the other two suddenly returned underneath me and opened fire from a spot where I could not see them, one coming within a hundred yards. Almost at the same moment that they attacked, four enemy scouts came diving out of the clouds, two of them firing as they dived at me. I turned on the nearer of the two-seaters and, firing forty rounds at him from the side, managed to shoot him down. I then went straight at the four scouts, opening fire on one that was coming straight head-on. He swerved slightly at the last, and flashed by me. I ducked away into a cloud to consider the situation for a moment, but in the mist, in my excitement, I lost control of my machine and fell in a spinning nose-dive for quite a distance. When I flattened out at last, the enemy scouts had flown away, but there beneath me, still slowly spinning to his fate, was my second two-seater. Three of the missing scouts now appeared some distance above me. I decided it was not a very healthy spot, and made away for home, perfectly content with having added two more Hun scalps to my score.

It was great flying-weather, and next day I had four fights in forty-five minutes. I could have had more, but had to return for want of fuel and ammunition. First of all, I spotted two of my favourite two-seaters doing their daily observations, some three miles on the German side of the lines. I was very careful now about the way I approached these people, and went at it in a more or less scientific manner. Climbing to just under the top of a cloud, where I was more or less invisible, I watched them carefully for five whole minutes as they went back and forth on their beat, and I carefully figured out just where I could catch them when they were nearest our lines. I also kept a very close eye on some enemy fighting patrols lurking in the distance. Picking a moment when they were well away, I flew over some more sheltering clouds, then came down and dashed at the two Huns. I managed to get twenty rounds into the nearer one, and pretty good shots they were, too, but nothing seemed to happen. At least nothing happened to the Hun, but something went wrong with my engine, and fearing it would fail me altogether, I broke off the fight and made for home.

Just after I made our lines, the engine began running perfectly, so I went back for my two-seaters. Only one of them remained. This convinced me that the other machine had been hit badly enough to make him descend. The one left behind was very wary, and I saw I could not get within two miles of him. So I gave him up as a bad job, and flew up and down the lines until I discovered another pair of two-seaters. These also proved to be shy and I chased them well back into their own country. It is discouraging work, and very aggravating, to chase machines that will not fight. For my part, I find that I get in a tremendous temper and am very apt to run unnecessary risks when I meet another enemy. It is a case of anything to relieve one's feelings.

The last twenty minutes of the three-quarters of an hour were spent first in stalking an enemy scout, that also escaped; then the two machines I had previously attacked in my second fight, some minutes before. But again I was unable to get within close range of them, although I finally flew above and got between them and their own aerodrome. I dashed at the two head-on, but finished my ammunition before I had done any damage.

In the afternoon I had three more fights, the first one being very unsuccessful from my point of view, but certainly a very exciting affair. I was out with my own patrol, six machines strong, and we had not been on the lines very long before we met up with a lone Hun two-seater. From a distance he looked like one of the shy fellows I had been chasing most of the morning, and I led the patrol

132

straight at him, quite confident in my own mind that he was going to be an easy victim. I was convinced of this when at first he appeared inclined to run away. I opened fire at him at 200 yards, whereupon a marvellous thing happened. The German pilot turned in a flash and came head-on into the six of us, opening fire with two guns. Much to our amazement, he flew right through the centre of our formation. The unexpected audacity of the Hun caught us entirely off our guard. It was a bad bit of work for us to let him go right through us, and we were all deeply disgusted. We turned on the fellow with all the fury there was in us, but he was quite ready for us. We seemed to be fighting very badly, and the honours were not coming our way. The fight lasted about three minutes, and during that time I, for one, was caught badly by the German. While trying to correct a stoppage in my gun, he turned on me and got in a very fierce burst of fire, some of the bullets passing close to my body. He also got one of the others a few seconds later trying to do the same thing, and then, to cap the climax, he turned away, broke off the combat, and escaped as free as a bird, with probably only a few bullet-holes in his machine. He must have been a very fine pilot and a very brave man, for he put up a wonderful fight, and I have not the slightest hesitation in saying he probably enjoyed it much more than we did.

A little later I was flying around when I saw dead beneath me a green-and-black machine, with huge black crosses painted on it. It was one of the new type of enemy scouts, and, as I later discovered, had a very good man piloting it. I dived at him, but he did a great turn, climbing at the same time, and by a clever manœuvre managed to get directly behind me. I had a hard time getting rid of him, as he had me in a very awkward position, and every second for several minutes I expected that one of his bullets which were passing close by me would find its mark.

But even in a perilous time like this my sense of humour would out, and I thought of a verse from "The Lobster Quadrille":

> *"Won't you walk a little faster?"*
> *Said a whiting to a snail;*
> *"There's a porpoise close behind me,*
> *And he's treading on my tail!"*

I did not like that Hun porpoise at all, and he was treading on my tail like the very shadow of Death itself. However, he made a slight mistake on one of our turns, and a few seconds later I got into a position where the fight began anew on rather different terms. For several minutes we flew around in a circle, both getting in occasional bursts of fire. Out of the corner of my eye I saw some scarlet German machines approaching, so I snatched at an opportunity that suddenly appeared and escaped.

A few minutes later, on returning to that spot, I saw that the Hun scouts had found another one of our machines by itself, and were all attacking it. So I came down from above and created a momentary diversion by opening fire with my last ten rounds, and thus gave the British machine a chance to escape. Our pilot slid speedily out of the fray.

We were up late that night attending a show given for the squadron by a travelling troupe of concert people from

134

the Army Service Corps. It was past midnight when I got to bed, and I was up again at four, having an early-morning job on hand. I will never forget the orderly who used to wake me in those days. He positively enjoyed it.

After a cup of hot tea and a biscuit, four of us left the ground shortly after five. The sun in the early mornings, shining in such direct rays from the east, makes it practically impossible to see in that direction, so that these dawn adventures were not much of a pleasure. It meant that danger from surprise was very great, for the Huns, coming from the east with the sun at their back, could see us when we couldn't see them. At any rate, one doesn't feel one's best at dawn, especially when one has had only four hours' sleep. This was the case on this bright May morning, and to make matters worse there was quite a ground mist. The sun, reflecting on this, made seeing in any direction very difficult.

We had been doing a patrol up and down the line for an hour and a quarter, at a very high altitude where it was cruelly cold, so I decided to lead the patrol down lower. There did not seem to be an enemy in the air, and for a moment I think my vigilance was relaxed. I had begun to dream a bit, when suddenly a burst of machine-gun fire awakened me to the fact that there was a war on. Not even taking time to look from whence it all came, I pulled my machine up and turned it like lightning, looking over my shoulder during the whirl. This instinctive manœuvre saved my life. An enemy machine, painted a beautiful silver, was coming vertically down at me firing. He just missed me with his bullets, and, "zooming" up again, he made a second dive. This time I pulled my machine back, and with

135

my nose to the sky, I fired at the Hun as he came down. I then flew sidewise and evaded him that way. It had been a clear case of surprise so far as I was concerned, and I had a very narrow squeak from disaster.

Altogether, there were five Huns in the attacking force, against the four of us. We were flying in diamond formation, and the pilot bringing up our rear had seen the Huns just before the attack, but not in time to warn us. Counting the five enemy pilots, he wondered which one of us was going to be attacked by two Huns instead of one? The next moment he saw the Germans split up as they dived at us, and he was the unfortunate one to draw the two. It was a lucky thing for the rest of us, taken wholly by surprise, that we each had but a single machine to deal with. Our rearguard was better prepared, and although we all had our troubles, we managed to clear away without injury.

Next day we had rather a dramatic touch. After the morning's work we were sitting at luncheon and the second course had just been served, when a telephone message came through that two enemy machines were at work on the lines. They were directing artillery fire of several hostile batteries on some of our important points. The request came through from the front line to send somebody out at once and drive the undesirables away. Talk about Wellington at the battle of Waterloo! This had that beaten in every way. We felt like a lot of firemen, and in a very few minutes after we got the message another pilot and I were out over the trenches. Five minutes later we were engaged in deadly combat with the two enemy machines. They had seen us as we approached. We were hungry and were anxious to get back to our muttons. So there was no shilly-shallying about the fight—it was a case of going in and finishing it in the shortest possible order. So the two of us waded in side by side, opening fire on the rear enemy. With our first burst of fire, it dived on its nose, did a couple of turns as it fell, and finally crashed into a field beside the river. We then turned our attention to Hun Number 2, but he was a mile away by this time and winging it for home as fast as ever he could. We were willing to waste ten minutes more away from the festive board to have a go at him, but he showed no sign of returning, and we streaked home to our interrupted meal. It had all been very short and sweet, and most successful.

I had now come to the conclusion that to be successful in fighting in the air, two things were required above all others. One was accuracy in shooting, and the second was to use one's head and take no unnecessary risks. Consequently my plans from about this time forward were to take a minimum of risks, and whenever things looked at all doubtful or bad, immediately to make my escape and wait patiently for another opportunity. The patience part in carrying out this campaign was the hardest, but I managed to control myself, and found it much more effective than constantly blundering into danger like a bull in a china-shop.

For instance, one day I saw a single enemy scout flying at a tremendous altitude. I climbed up carefully some distance from him, and got between him and the sun; then, waiting until he was heading in exactly the opposite direction, I came down with tremendous speed and managed to slip underneath him without even being seen. I could make out each mark on the bottom of his machine as I crept closer and closer. My gun was all ready, but I withheld its fire until I came to the range I wanted—inside of 20 yards. It was rather delicate work flying so close under the swift Hun, but he had no idea that I was in existence, much less sitting right below him. I carefully picked out the exact spot where I knew the pilot was sitting, took careful aim, and fired. Twenty tracer bullets went into that spot. The machine immediately lurched to one side and fell.

I had quickly to skid my machine to one side to avoid being hit by the falling Hun. After he had passed me a little way, I saw him smoking. Then he burst into flames. That pilot never knew what happened to him. Death came to him from nowhere.

Shortly after this, learning by accident that a patrol from another squadron was going across to take photographs, I offered to accompany them as escort, and was accepted. The anti-aircraft fire that day was really terrible. I flew well above the photographers and was more or less out of reach of the "Archies," but the other machines were getting it hammer and tongs. All got through the barrage, however, and we proceeded to get our pictures. Then we headed straight for home. About this time I noticed several of the "Little Red Devils" flying about underneath us, so I watched them carefully, suspecting they were climbing to attack some of the photography machines. I also began to climb so as to be practically out of sight in the blue sky, and I managed to fool them altogether. Two of the devils soon came at one of our machines, and at the same time I dived into them. One of the pair turned away, but I managed to get in a good shot at the second one at 30 yards. He immediately flew out of control, and I watched him falling for what seemed to be a long time. I was now down to the level of the photographers and remained with them for the rest of the trip. The "Archies" gave us another hot greeting as we recrossed the lines. I kept dodging about as quickly as I could, for the fire was too close to be pleasant. Shells were bursting everywhere. There was no use turning to the right, for you would stick your nose into two or three exploding shells in that direction. And there was no use turning to the left, for three or four would be bursting there. They seemed to fill every nook and corner of the air. I was greatly tempted to put my engine full out and leave the patrol to get home by itself, but I did not. I stuck with the heavier machines, dodging around them like a young sparrow among a lot of crows.

The photographic machines were badly hit, and three of them had been so damaged they could not be used again. My own machine was hit in several places, and I never looked back upon that volunteer excursion as one of the pleasant experiences in my young life. This was the last fighting I had for two weeks, as the next day I went to England on two weeks' leave.

CHAPTER 13

WHEN I LEFT for my leave to England, I was not very keen on going. The excitement of the chase had a tight hold on my heartstrings, and I felt that the only thing I wanted was to stay right at it and fight and fight and fight in the air. I don't think I was ever happier in my life. It seemed that I had found the one thing I loved above all others. To me it was not a business or a profession, but just a wonderful game. To bring down a machine did not seem to me to be killing a man; it was more as if I was just destroying a mechanical target, with no human being in it. Once or twice the idea that a live man had been piloting the machine would occur and recur to me, and it would worry me a bit. My sleep would be spoiled perhaps for a night. I did not relish the idea even of killing Germans, yet, when in a combat in the air, it seemed more like any other kind of sport, and to shoot down a machine was very much the same as if one were shooting down clay pigeons. One had the great satisfaction of feeling that one had hit the target and brought it down; that one was victorious again.

When I reached England, however, I found I was in a very nervous condition. I could not be still. After a week there, in which I enjoyed myself tremendously, I found I was getting quieter, and realized that my leave was probably doing me a world of good. My last week of leave I enjoyed without stint, every minute seeming better than the one before. To make it still more ideal, I did not have the usual dread of going back to France—I was looking forward to it. I realized that this short rest had quieted my nerves and had left me in a much better state of health, so that when the two weeks were up and the day came for my return I gladly got on the train leaving Charing Cross, and all day looked forward to my return to the squadron. By great luck, I managed to catch an automobile going in my direction from Boulogne, and arrived at the aerodrome the same night I had left London. I felt like a small boy returning home for his holidays. I was plied with questions as to what "good old England" looked like, what I had done and what was happening in "Blighty"; and in my turn I was full of questions as to what had happened in the squadron while I was away. Many things had: several people had been killed, and quite a number of Hun machines had been shot down by our pilots. A great many exciting and a great many amusing fights in the air were related.

It was typical of the attitude of these comrades of mine that when a man had been in an exceedingly tight corner and had managed to squeeze out of it, it was later related as a very amusing, not as a very terrible, incident, and as the narrator would tell his story the others would shriek with laughter at the tale of how nearly he had been hit and how "scared" he had been. It was such a wonderful way to take life that, upon looking back at it, I feel that nothing the future can ever hold for me can excel those wonderful days. Face to face with death every day, but always with the best of comrades and the most tried of friends, it has left a wonderful memory with me.

The day after rejoining the squadron, I did my first job at 9 o'clock in the morning. I must admit I felt very funny in the machine. I seemed to have lost all "feel" of it and could not turn or fly it properly at all. However, that day I had two jobs, and by the end of the second luckily had run into no exciting episodes.

Then came the reaction. I felt a wonderful thrill at being back in the air again, and handling my beloved Nieuport. It seemed that nothing was dangerous, and that to throw this machine about in the air was just the best sport that had ever been invented. I remember racing along close to the ground, seeing how close I could make my wing-tips come to the sheds and trees without hitting them. It was all just a wonderful thrill, and no thought of peril entered my head. That evening I went up and spent an hour in flying, just for the pure pleasure of it. Life was as sweet as it could be, and I saw the world through rose-coloured glasses.

That night the romance of our life at the front was brought home to me again. We spent the evening after dark standing around a piano, while one of our number played popular songs, the remainder singing in loud and varied keys, going on the principle that if you cannot sing, at least you can make a joyful noise.

About 9 o'clock a party of ten others arrived from a squadron stationed near us, and we had more music and songs with them. Everybody was happy; flying and fighting had been forgotten for the moment, and war was a thing far, far away. Toward the end of the party we went to the farmyard near by, appropriated some small pigs only a few months old, and placed them in the room of one of our

143

pilots who was dining out. Then, about 11 o'clock, when he had come back, we went into the next room to listen through the thin partition to his remarks when he entered his pig-filled boudoir. In a small space about 10 by 6 over fifteen of us were jammed anxiously waiting for the climax of the evening. In the other room the little pigs were grunting away merrily, and it was all we could do to keep from roaring with laughter. It was pitch black, and with the funny little squeals coming through the partition there would occasionally be a bit of a scamper, for although we at first placed the pigs on the bed, on looking over the partition I saw they were moving around the room in formation, one of their number evidently having assigned himself the position of leader of the pork patrol.

Unfortunately, the episode fell through miserably, as the pigs took up a station near the door, and when the owner of the room returned and opened it he walked across to light his lamp. The pigs, seeing the opening before he had seen them, made a dash and managed to get out, with a great chorus of squealing. They hid under the huts, and it took the rest of us several hours to find them and take them back to their mother.

After going to bed, I was awakened by one of my dogs scampering out of the hut. I listened for a minute and heard voices outside, got up and walked out in my pyjamas. It was a perfect moonlight night, without a breath of wind, and bright as could be. Outside two or three others were standing in pyjamas, and after asking what was the matter I was told there was a German machine overhead. Listening carefully, I could hear the beat of a Mercédès engine about a mile away. We could not see the Hun, but could

Major William A. Bishop *(Courtesy of the Royal Canadian Air Force)*

Bishop standing next to his favourite Nieuport 17
(Courtesy of the Royal Canadian Air Force)

top right Lieutenant Bishop wearing the "O" and single wing of an
RFC Observer
(Courtesy of the Royal Canadian Air Force)

right Bishop's post-war partner, Billy Barker, right, about to take the
Prince of Wales for a flight during World War I
(Royal Canadian Air Force photograph)

A Nieuport 17 in flight over the lines
(Official U.S. Air Force photograph)

top right An SE-5A, British-built scout of the type flown by Bishop
(Courtesy of the National Archives)

right The famous Sopwith "Camel," contemporary of the SE-5A
(National Defence photograph, Canada)

"The Red Baron"— Rittmeister Manfred Von Richthofen — was the leading ace of both sides with eighty confirmed victories. Like Bishop, he too entered the war as a cavalry officer
(Courtesy of the National Archives)

The enemy Albatross D-V *(Official U.S. Air Force photo)*

The Fokker D-VII, probably the greatest plane to come out of the war.
Bishop tried his hand on a captured one like this
(Courtesy of the National Archives)

Aerial view of the Ypres battlefield *(Official U.S. Air Force photo)*

hear him quite distinctly as he flew past. Then came the explosions as a few bombs were dropped, and then more explosions as the anti-aircraft guns located the moonlight marauder and began to fire. We could see little bursts of flame as the shells exploded high in the air. It was a beautiful show. The light was too bright even to see the stars, but these fierce little bursts of flame dotted the sky first in one spot, then in another, and gradually travelled in a line toward the trenches, as the enemy made in that direction. He got away safely, however, and we returned to bed.

In our home in a beautiful green orchard, our life was full of the most extraordinary contrasts. One minute we were as far removed from the war as if we were in South America, and an hour later we would be fighting for our lives or carrying on in some way directly connected with the mad world-struggle. It all added to the lure of life and somehow made the real fighting, when it came, seem less real and tragic.

CHAPTER 14

THE SECOND DAY after my return I began another three months of strenuous battles. The squadron had been assigned a new kind of work to do, in addition to regular patrol. This lasted throughout a great part of the month of June, and gave us some very strenuous mornings, although the afternoons were generally easier.

My first fight occurred in the early morning, about 7 o'clock, when I was leading a patrol. The clouds were very low, being about 4000 feet, the lower part of each cloud having a thin hanging mist about it. This made it possible to fly just in the mist, without being seen at more than 200 yards.

I had been gazing far into enemy territory, and suddenly saw five enemy scouts dive out of the clouds, then, after coming in our direction for a moment or two, dive back into the mist. I thought they were trying to surprise us, and crawled up as close to the clouds as I could, heading in their direction. Suddenly they loomed up just in front of us, and evidently were more surprised than we were. I only managed to get in a short burst, when my machine gun jammed hopelessly; but the remainder of the patrol gave chase to the Huns as they turned to run and scattered them helter-skelter. One man appeared to be hit, and one of my men went after him in a vertical dive to

147

1000 feet from the ground, when the enemy suddenly regained control, and darted across his own lines, escaping.

Later in the day I went out by myself, and, flying over Vimy Ridge and Lens, was watching a ground battle taking place there, when suddenly I saw a single scout of the enemy underneath me. He did not see me, and I dived at him and managed to fall into the much-desired position just behind his tail. I opened fire, and my tracer bullets could be seen going all around the pilot's seat. I had considerable speed from my dive, and was going much faster than he was, so whirled past him. Then, to avoid getting him behind me, I "zoomed" up and, after reaching 500 feet above, made a quick turn to see what had happened. To this day I have not the faintest idea what happened. My enemy entirely disappeared from view. I looked all around underneath, and everywhere else, but could not see him. Later, I telephoned to the anti-aircraft batteries and infantry stations near the front-line trenches, but they could give no information. That particular Hun must have dissolved.

Ten minutes later I had another fight. I had seen, some distance away, two of the enemy. They were fighting machines, so I reconnoitred carefully, and a little later discovered two more Huns were flying 2000 feet above them. I climbed up, and looked carefully from a distance at these; then climbed a little higher, with the idea of attacking them, when I suddenly saw two more Huns 3000 feet above the second pair. It was a layer formation, and a favourite trap of the Huns, their idea being that our machines would come along and attack the lower pair, in which case the middle pair would come down on top of them, leaving the highest pair in reserve. This had been tried innumerable times, and had been more or less successful, but, long since, our people had become wise and always watched for anything of that sort. By pure luck, that morning, I saw the top pair, and, flying away off to one side, climbed as fast as I could until 2000 feet above them; then followed along. I was quite certain there was no fourth pair, and also knew that the third pair would be very keen on watching underneath them to see that their comrades were not attacked. It was a case of the trappers trapped; and, successful on this occasion, I was always on the look-out for the same sort of thing after that day, and succeeded in bringing down some of the top-side people on several other occasions.

This day I dived down at the top pair, one of which was flying directly behind the other. I did not touch my trigger until I was fifty yards from him; then opened a stiff fire. This machine, as on the previous time I had used a similar trick, knew nothing of what was coming to him at all. He also probably never knew what hit him, because, slipping to one side, his machine went into a spin and fell completely out of control. I did not wait to attack the other man, as I was underneath him; and by the time he had turned to see what was happening, I was a quarter of a mile away, and going for home as fast as possible. It was the first machine to my credit since my return from England, and I was greatly pleased.

By this time I had become very ambitious, and was hoping to get a large number of machines officially credited to me before I left France. With this object in view, I planned many little expeditions of my own, and, with the use of great patience, I was very successful in one or two.

The next day I was out with my patrol again in the morning, and met six enemy scouts. There were six of us as well, but in the earlier part of the "scrap" which immediately followed, my gun, which seemed to be causing me a lot of trouble, again jammed, and I signalled to the others that I had to leave the fight. I dived away, and landed on an aerodrome near by to correct the jam.

Three-quarters of an hour later I was again in the air, but could not find the patrol, so I flew up over Vimy Ridge. There was one of my old friends, a big, fat two-seater, and I went after him with joy in my soul. Three times I managed to get in a burst of fire, diving once from straight above and once from either side, but I did not seem to be able to hit him at all.

Glancing suddenly over my shoulder, I saw two enemy scouts coming to the rescue from above. They had been sitting away up in the blue sky, in order to protect this machine, and, luckily for me, had not seen me sooner. I cleared off, and carefully thought how I was to get my revenge. Nothing in the world but that fat two-seater attracted my attention. I was annoyed at having missed him, after such good chances, and was determined I was at least going to have another good go at him before giving up. The only trouble was the two enemy scouts above, and I did not know how to get rid of them. They had seen me, and probably had their eye on me at the moment.

I flew away, and came back in five minutes. Luck was with me; another one of our machines had flown slightly above the two enemy scouts, who had turned and fled from him. He had chased them, and they had made a détour, evading him. All this I took in at a glance, and saw that they were trying to get back to protect their two-seater comrade, and had no desire to fight, themselves. Seeing my opportunity, as the two-seater did not seem to know that the scouts had temporarily deserted him, I dived at him again, and this time closed up to within 50 yards before opening fire. Then, taking an accurate aim, I pulled the trigger. I can remember to this day how carefully I aimed that time. I was dead behind him, and I picked out the finest point in the pilot's body where I wanted my bullets to hit. The observer in the two-seater ceased firing at me a moment before I opened, and began to work frantically at his gun. It had the jamming habit, too. A few rounds were enough. The machine put its nose down, dived vertically a short distance, then went into an uncontrolled spinning dive, and I watched it as it fell racing down toward the ground, with the engine full on. As is always the case, it seemed to take an age before it reached the ground. Finally, it crashed into the centre of a village, striking between two houses.

Ten minutes later I had climbed up and was above the two scouts, so decided to give them at least a scare. I opened fire at long range, and, for a moment, thought I had hit one of them. He went into a spin, but 2000 feet below flattened out and flew away. The other one climbed and I could not catch him, so turned and flew north.

Another two-seater, who had been flying along the lines, was now 3000 feet above me. I opened fire at him from underneath, at very long range, but, of course, could not hit, the range being too long.

Many exciting fights occurred with the machines doing artillery observation. They were a very difficult proposition. They knew for a certainty they would be attacked, and would fly in threes and fours, or more, going about on their beat all together, and helping their own lines, and at a height of 3000 feet. It made it very difficult for us to attack, as, the height being low, we would have to make a dash across the lines at them, and then back again. Over and over again one would carefully figure out where they would be nearest the lines, then, at that moment, dash across at full speed. The enemy, immediately upon seeing the anti-aircraft shells burst around you, would turn east and fly toward home, going as fast as they could, and at the same time losing height. It meant that really to destroy or damage them, one had to fly ten or twelve miles in to catch them; then they would only be at a height of some 500 or 1000 feet. This was our task. The anti-aircraft fire was terrific, going in not as bad as coming back; but the moment we turned to come home all the guns in the neighbourhood would open at us, and, if we were low enough, we would also be subjected to the most intense machine-gun fire from the ground.

This did not occur once a week; it was a thing that happened to each one of us three and four times, or even more, in the course of a morning's work, and was the most trying job we had to do. Most of the fights followed the same lines, three or four of us crossing at full speed, zigzagging slightly in our course to upset the aim of the "Archies," and then following closely the enemy machines, which were all the time directing a steady machine-gun fire at us. Our object was more to frighten them away

152

than really to bring them down. Then would come a quick turn, and a dash back home. This would be very hard to do. One would turn suddenly to the right or left, trying to evade the bursting shells, but they were cracking on all sides. It would seem that one could not possibly get through them, and the thought that one little bit of shell in the engine would put the whole machine out of business was enough to give anybody nerves. As it was, we were nearly always hit by small fragments, but this was considered nothing, and, of course, no reason for not liking the job. My previous experience in escorting the photography machines had taught me that other people have to stand anti-aircraft fire as well as ourselves, and for them, being larger and slower, it is a thousand times worse.

CHAPTER 15

MY RECORD of machines brought down was now in the vicinity of twenty, and I saw I had a rare chance of really getting a lot before going on my next leave—at the end of my second three months at the front.

With this object in view I planned an expedition into the enemy country, to attack an enemy aerodrome. I had carefully thought it out, and came to the conclusion that if one could get to an aerodrome when there were some machines on the ground and none in the air, it would be an easy matter to shoot them down the moment they would attempt to come up. It would be necessary for them to take off straight into the wind, if there was a strong wind at all, so I could not be surprised that way, and would be able to hit them if I came low enough, before they would get a chance to manoeuvre or turn out of my way.

I planned this expedition after much thought, and set it for June 2nd, as that was to be my day off. Dawn was the hour I considered advisable, as there would be very few machines in the air, and I would have a great chance of evading trouble on the way to the aerodrome. I spent my spare moments, the next few days, arranging the details.

In the meantime I had several more fights. On May 31st I went out in the morning about 8 o'clock, and the sky seemed deserted. However, I crossed over into enemy territory, and in a few minutes sighted two machines. They

155

were flying south. I followed, and suddenly they began to spiral down. Apparently they had just finished their time in the air, and were coming down to land. So I flew as quickly as I could, and reached the nearest one, whom I attacked, firing a burst from 50 yards range. I missed him completely, I think. He turned, and we had quite a fight, lasting four or five minutes. Luckily, his companion had not seen us; and had kept on going down. My opponent seemed a very good man, and every time, just as I thought I was going to get in a burst of fire, he would make some clever manœuvre and evade me altogether, with the result that I was having a very hard time myself, and had to keep my eyes open so that he would not get a good shot at me. For a moment or two I was a bit worried, but suddenly I managed to get slightly behind him, and at a favourable angle, only 15 yards away. I pulled the trigger, and his machine fell out of control. Much pleased, I waited over the spot to see him crash—which he did.

The next morning, remembering my bad shooting in the beginning of this fight, I spent some extra time on the target at the aerodrome. During that day I went out no less than four times, looking for a fight, but in only one case did I even get near enough to open fire at an enemy machine; that time only getting within 150 yards of it. Two of us went after him, but, as usual, he decided that it was not healthy, and putting his engine full on, dived away as quickly as he could go, to the tune of our machine guns behind him. However, it had no result except to frighten him. He did not return. The remainder of that day all the German machines seemed very nervous, and we could not get within range of any of them.

Now came the day planned for my expedition. I wrote my name on the blackboard, the night before, to be called at 3 o'clock, and sat down for the last time to consider exactly if the job was worth the risk. However, as nothing like it had been done before, I knew that I would strike the Huns by surprise, and, considering that, I decided the risk was not nearly so great as it seemed, and that I might be able to get four or five more machines to my credit, in one great swoop.

At 3 o'clock I was called and got up. It was pitch-black. I dressed, and went in to tell two of my friends that I was off. They were not entirely in favour of the expedition, and said so again. Notwithstanding this, I went on to the aerodrome, and got away just as the first streaks of dawn were showing in the upper sky.

I flew straight across the lines, toward the aerodrome I had planned to attack, and coming down low, decided to carry out my plan and stir them up with a burst of machine-gun fire into their hangar sheds. But, on reaching the place, I saw there was nothing on the ground. Everyone must have been either dead asleep or else the station was absolutely deserted. Greatly disappointed, I decided I would try the same stunt some other day on another aerodrome, which I would have to select.

In the meantime, for something to do, I flew along low over the country, in the hope of coming on some camp or group of troops so as to scatter them. I felt that the danger was nil, as most of the crews of the guns which ordinarily would fire at me would still be asleep, and I might as well give any Huns I could find a good fright. I was in rather a bad temper at having my carefully laid plan fall through

157

so quickly, and nothing would have pleased me better than to have run across a group of fat Huns drilling in a field, or something of that sort. However, nothing appeared, and I was just thinking of turning and going home, or of climbing up to see if there were some Huns in the upper sky, when ahead, and slightly to one side of me, I saw the sheds of another aerodrome. I at once decided that here was my chance, although it was not a very favourable one, as the aerodrome was pretty far back from the lines. To make good my escape from this place would not be as easy as I had hoped. Furthermore, I was not even certain where I was, and that was my greatest worry, as I was a bit afraid that if I had any bad fights I might have trouble in finding my way back. Scurrying along close to the ground, zigzagging here and there, one's sense of direction becomes slightly vague.

Another half-minute and I was over the aerodrome, about 300 feet up. On the ground were seven German machines, and in my first glance I saw that some of them actually had their engines running. Mechanics were standing about in groups. Then I saw a thing which surprised me very much—six of the machines were single-seaters, and one a two-seater. I was not very anxious for the two-seater to come up to attack me, as in taking off he would have a certain amount of protection from behind, with his observer, while the single-seater could have none. However, in this, luck also favoured me, as the two-seater did not move at all.

I pointed my nose toward the ground, and opened fire with my gun, scattering the bullets all around the machines, and coming down to 50 feet in doing so. I do not know

158

how many men I hit, or what damage was done, except
that one man, at least, fell, and several others ran to pick
him up. Then, clearing off to one side, I watched the fun.
I had forgotten by this time that they would, of course,
have machine guns on the aerodrome, and as I was laughing
to myself, as they tore around in every direction on the
ground, like people going mad or rabbits scurrying about,
I heard the old familiar rattle of the quick-firers on me.
I did not dare go too far away, however, as then I would
not be able to catch the machines as they left the ground,
so turning quickly and twisting about, I did my best to
evade the fire from the ground. Looking at my planes,
I saw that the guns were doing pretty good shooting. There
were several holes in them already, and this made me turn
and twist all the more. Then one machine suddenly began
to "taxi" off down the aerodrome. It increased its speed
quickly, and I immediately tore down after it. I managed
to get close on its tail, when it was just above the ground,
and opened fire from dead behind it. There was no chance
of missing, and I was as cool as could be. Just fifteen
rounds, and it side-slipped to one side, then crashed on the
aerodrome underneath. I was now keyed up to the fight,
and turning quickly, saw another machine just off the
ground. Taking careful aim at it, I fired from longer
range than before, as I did not want to waste the time of
going up close. For one awful moment I saw my bullets
missing, and aimed still more carefully, all the time striving
to get nearer. The Hun saw I was catching him up, and
pushed his nose down; then, gazing over his shoulder at
the moment I was firing at him, he crashed into some trees
near the aerodrome. I think I hit him just before he came

159

to the trees, as my tracers were then going in an accurate line.

I again turned toward the aerodrome. This time my heart sank, because two machines were taking off at the same time, and in slightly different directions. It was the one thing I had dreaded. There was not much wind, and it was possible for them to do this. I had made up my mind, before, that if they attempted to do this I would immediately make good my escape, but I had counted on being higher. However, true to my intention, I began to climb. One of the enemy machines luckily climbed away at some distance, while the other made up straight after me. At 1000 feet, and only a few hundred yards from the aerodrome, I saw that he was catching me, so turned on him and opened fire. We made about two circuits around each other, neither getting a very good shot, but in the end I managed to get in a short burst of fire, and his machine went crashing to the ground, where it lay in a field, a few hundred yards from the aerodrome.

The fourth machine then came up, and I opened fire on him. I was now greatly worried as to how I was to get away, as I was using up all my ammunition, and there seemed to be no end to the number of machines coming up. I was afraid that other machines from other aerodromes would also come in answer to telephone calls, and wanted to get away as quickly as I could. But there was no chance of running from this man—he had me cold—so I turned at him savagely, and, in the course of a short fight, emptied the whole of my last drum at him. Luckily, at the moment I finished my ammunition, he also seemed to have had enough of it, as he turned and flew away. I seized my opportunity, climbed again, and started for home.

To my dismay I discovered four enemy scouts above me. I was terrified that they would see me, so flew directly underneath them, for some time—almost a mile, I should think—going directly south. Then, deciding that I must do something, I took the bit in my teeth and slipped away. They did not atempt to attack me at all, so I am not sure whether they even saw me or not.

I now headed in the approximate direction of our lines, and flew in rather a dazed state toward them. I had not had any breakfast, and was feeling very queer at my stomach. The excitement, and the reaction afterward, had been a bit too much, as well as the cold morning air. It seemed, once or twice, that my head was going around and around, and that something must happen. For the only time in my life it entered my thoughts that I might lose my senses in a moment, and go insane. It was a horrible feeling, and I also had the terrible sensation that I would suffer from nausea any minute. I was not at all sure where I was, and furthermore did not care. The thrills and ex-ultation I had at first felt had all died away, and nothing seemed to matter but this awful feeling of dizziness and the desire to get home and on the ground.

By the time I reached the aerodrome, however, I felt much better, and flew over our still sleeping huts, firing off my signal lights frantically, to show them I had certainly had some success. I landed, and my sergeant immediately rushed out and asked me how many I had bagged. When I told him three, he was greatly pleased, and yelled it back to the mechanics who were waiting by the shed. Then, as I crawled out of my machine, I heard the remarks of the mechanics around me. They were looking it over. Everywhere it was shot about, bulletholes being in almost every part of it, although none, luckily, within 2 feet of where I sat. Parts of the machine were so badly damaged as to take a lot of repairing; but I used the same patched planes in the machine for some time afterward, and always felt great affection for it for pulling me through such a successful enterprise. I personally congratulated the man who had charge of my gun, suddenly realizing that if it had jammed at a critical moment what a tight corner I would have been in.

Within three or four hours I had received many congratulations upon this stunt, and what I had planned as merely a way of shooting down some more of the Huns I found the authorities considered a very successful expedition. It pleased me very much—and, of course, I have always kept the telegrams of congratulations which I received that day. At first I had been disappointed in the net result, for when I started out I had rather hoped they would all take off as the first machine did, and that I would be able to bag, at the very least, four. But, on looking back at it, I think I was over-optimistic, and was very lucky to have brought down as many as I did.

That afternoon I was still suffering from the excitement of the morning and, although tired out, could not sleep, so with one other man I climbed in my machine and flew about fifty miles south, to pay a visit to another of our aerodromes there. We left to return about 5 o'clock and had more excitement, as a rainstorm was coming up, and for the last ten minutes had to plough through a drizzle. It was pretty dreary work, and I was very glad to see the aerodrome again. An hour later I was sound asleep in my bed, and did not awaken until the next morning.

Next morning we had a most discouraging time. For several days there had not been many German machines on the lines, and we had been very successful in stopping them from doing their artillery work. But on this morning, when, with our usual confidence of finding only one or two, we slipped across the lines after them, we suddenly made out everywhere, groups of four or five; and, counting them up, I found there were no less than twenty-three German machines within three miles of the front. There were only three of us, so it was rather puzzling what to do. In some way we had to stop the machines from doing artillery work, and it was not a very pleasant prospect for three to pile into the middle of over twenty, with the likelihood of still more coming from other directions. However, we stayed just on the German side of the line, and they did not seem very anxious to attack us. So, whenever two or three got separated from the others, we pretended to go near them, and they would shy away toward the rest of their machines. It was terribly annoying to have to sit there and see so many fat Huns go unmolested, and after we landed we agreed that if it ever happened again, one of us would go back, get more machines to help, and then we would engage the lot in a real battle royal. So many times we could not find any of them, when we were just dying for a fight; now they were in such huge numbers it would be folly to mix up with them.

We managed to have three short goes at different artillery machines in the course of half an hour next day, but they were not "having any," however, and turned away and fled toward home.

Another time, while flying on the lines, my engine suddenly stopped dead. Nothing I could do had any effect on it, and I glided back toward home. At first I was a bit afraid I would not even clear the shell area, and it would mean crashing into some deep hole, but there was a slight wind behind me, and with the help of this I glided on and on into clear country, where there was an aerodrome.

In one week I had no less than three engine failures, although I have hardly ever had one at any other time. But, as luck would have it, I was always able to glide down and just reach the same aerodrome. I got to know it quite well by the end of the week.

On June 8th fortune favoured me. I had had two indecisive combats, when, to my great joy, I saw in the distance another layer formation of six Huns in groups of two. So I manœuvred again, to attack the top pair. After creeping up slowly and carefully behind one of them, I opened fire, and he went straight away into a spinning nose-dive, which he could not come out of, and crashed into the ground. The other machine of the top layer saw me, but had no desire to fight, and dived away immediately toward the rest of his formation. I pointed my nose down at him and fired, but he was too far away and escaped.

This was again my day off, so I had deserted my own part of the lines and flown away up north where the battle of Messines was raging, and I had heard there were more German machines up in that direction. It was a good tip, and I was glad I had come.

A little later I saw the same or another formation of

four, flying about in a group. I did not feel like going down and getting into the middle of them, so I stayed above and tried the old game of diving and coming up again, just to worry them. It evidently did, as they only stood for it twice, and then, losing height, made away as fast as they could go.

Over a week passed now before I had another fight at all. Many times I sighted enemy aircraft, but they were always in the distance, and after a hot chase I would have to give it up. Then would come the disagreeable return journey against the anti-aircraft fire. By this time I was getting to hate the German guns, as they often caught me at low altitude and made the way home so nasty. One night when a shell burst near me, I happened to see the flash of the gun that was firing, and as it was almost directly beneath me, I threw my machine out of control, with a sudden inspiration, and let it fall for several thousand feet. Then, about two thousand feet from the ground, I opened fire at the battery on the ground. I was too high to see just what effect my fire had, but it evidently silenced them, and from later results certainly annoyed them very much, because every time I crossed the line on "Blue Nose," this gun would open fire fiercely, concentrating on me, no matter how many other machines were in the air.

About five miles south of this position, on another day, I was flying at a height of 2000 feet, and saw another "Archie" firing, so I dived down to about 500 feet from the ground and scattered some flaming bullets around him. This battery also gave "Blue Nose" special attention from that day on.

It became a favourite habit of ours, about this time,

when there were no enemy machines up above, to come down low and attack the enemy trenches, from a height of from 100 to 500 feet. We would come down behind them, and, diving at them that way, open fire. It evidently frightened the Huns very much, from reports which we later heard.

In the June evenings the sky was a beautiful sight at sunset. If there was any wind blowing at all, the mist would be cleared away, and one could see almost to the end of the world. The ground was a riot of beautiful colours, and the dusty roads stretched away like long white ribbons.

CHAPTER 16

ALL OF JUNE was marked by the most perfect weather. The prevailing strong west winds stopped and a light breeze blew constantly from the east. Some days there was hardly a stir in the air. From dawn until sundown there was rarely a cloud in the sky, and although the heat-waves from the effect of the sun on the earth made flying very rough when near the ground, the days were wonderful, and we all felt like kings.

The mornings were very busy, as there were many calls to chase away hostile aircraft; but the afternoons we generally had to ourselves, and although it was necessary to stay right on the aerodrome, we found many amusements there.

The mess was situated on the very edge of the aerodrome and about twenty yards from a farmhouse, which possessed the most extraordinary farmyard I have ever seen. There were pigeons by the hundreds, and all kinds of fowl possible to imagine. A small pond in the middle of the farmyard afforded exercise and amusement for a flock of ducks. The raising of pigs, however, seemed to be the farmer's great specialty, and to these pigs I owe many amusing hours.

One afternoon, while looking through the farmyard, three of us decided to capture a large hog and trail it back to our quarters to shoo it into the room of a friend, who was at the moment sleeping. It was very easy to get the idea, but for inexperienced people it was a difficult job to get the porker.

After much mature deliberation we decided upon our victim—the largest and dirtiest one in the farmyard. It was lying half-buried in the mud near the pond, so with a few small pebbles we woke it up and frightened it on to dry land. Then began the chase. Two or three times we managed to corner it, but with a series of grunts and squeals it would charge one of us and make a clean getaway. Finally, seeing no other course open, we drove it into a small pig-pen which had only one outlet, an opening with a door covering it up to about 3 feet high. Opening the door, we shooed the pig in. It seemed to have no objection, and after it went one of my comrades with a rope. I carefully closed the door and bolted it from the outside, so that the pig could not force it open. Then, peering over the top, I witnessed a remarkable scene. The hog was now desperate and tearing around in a circle, squealing for all it was worth. My companion with the rope was trying to fix a noose on one of the hind legs. In doing so the pig kicked him, and turning, nearly knocked him over as it rushed past. The next phrase was a cry of. "Open the door and let me out." The airman was as badly frightened as the hog. Suddenly, with an extra squeal, our supposed victim made a leap up the door and, firmly fastening fore legs on to the top of it, worked up like a fat gymnast and fell over on the outside. By this time we were all laughing so much we could not interfere, and the pig got away.

Refusing to be beaten, we employed the services of a small French boy to help us, and he sneaked up behind another huge pig and fastened the rope to a hind leg. I then took hold of it to drive it home, but the poor beast, upon learning that he was tied up, had no intention of giving in, and immediately started away at a furious gallop, dragging me after it. Once around the farmyard we went, and half again, before I tripped on a stone and fell flat, and this pig also escaped. You see, I was having no luck with Huns.

Again the French boy came to our rescue and secured Mr. Pig, showing us how to drive it properly. This we did, and managed in the course of the next three-quarters of an hour to get the pig as far as the officers' quarters. To drive him in was a difficult matter, but with numerous assistants and much noise and shouting he finally entered, but, of course, the sleeping man had been awake long since. However, we got the pig into his room, where he was standing in his pyjamas, and to see a brave man frightened is a rare sight, but the rest of us had the chance then.

We took the pig into the mess to show him about, putting him in a little cage made of the fire-fender. He seemed quite satisfied here for a moment, then, deciding that he would like to get away, stuck his nose under the edge of the fire-fender, heaved it over his back, and with a disgusted grunt walked out. Feeling that he had earned his freedom, we let him go.

Every afternoon after that we found much fun out of the different animals in the farmyard. The French people were as pleased as we were until some of their ducks stopped laying, when, of course, we made good the value of the eggs that came not, and a great many more that would never have come.

One afternoon we secured three ducks and a lot of paint. One duck we painted with circles around it of red, white, and blue, just like the Allied markings on our machine. Of the other two we painted one red and one bright blue. They did not seem to appreciate it, but they were distinguished-looking ducks until about two months later, when they began to moult. Then one would see wandering through the grass a weird sight looking like a moth-eaten bird, a dirty scarlet in some places and a dirty white in others. It would be a horrible sight close to, but from a distance quite pretty, resembling some bird of paradise.

These ducks we tried hard to train, trying to teach them to walk on the ground in formations the same as we flew in the air. They were not very adept pupils, however, and, instead of walking at correct distances apart, would keep looking behind at us, and jostling into the men on the right and left.

One afternoon we got as many as sixteen ducks, and after giving them a good luncheon, by way of celebration for their outing, we put them on the roof of the mess, where they all sat in a stately row, quacking in spasms.

These incidents, though simple to tell now, at that time afforded us the greatest amusement, and as we were in no way cruel to the animals, the French people who owned them did not seem to mind.

However, perhaps one day we carried it a little far, as we tried to find the effect of alcohol upon the ducks. This was most amusing with two or three, because, although they did not like the first drop of it, when they had been forced to swallow that, they eagerly cried for more. Their return home was a ludicrous sight, sitting down on the ground every minute or two, and always walking in a "beaucoup" zigzag course, as the French would say. Once we got hold of the head drake of the flock, and, imagining him to be able to stand a little more than the rest, gave him a drop too much, with the result that he unfortunately died. It took quite a bit of broken French and more expressive French notes to reconcile the owner to his loss, but after a long and painful conversation of nearly half an hour he was in a better humour and, incidentally, a richer man. With that our attention to the ducks ceased, although by this time three-quarters of the flock had been painted various hues.

We now returned to the pigs, and found much fun with the smaller ones. These also were painted, and we always referred to their different parts in aeronautical terms, such as calling their legs their "undercarriage" and their bodies their "fuselage."

One little pig we had was a most successful picture. His legs and the underpart of his body were all painted scarlet, his nose and tail as well. On his back were huge red, white, and blue circles. The rest of his body was touched with red, white and blue, his ears being blue. It was very good paint, and the result was a beautifully shining, coloured pig. When he returned that night to the others they stood off and gazed at him in amazement, and for days would not associate with him. It was indeed a red-letter day in his existence, as he was certainly THE pig amongst all pigs.

Using the French boy on another occasion, we again

secured a large sow. Upon her we painted black crosses, a huge black cross on her nose, a little one on each ear, and a large one on each side. Then on her back we painted Baron von Richthofen. So that the other pigs would recognize that she was indeed a leader, we tied a leader's streamer on her tail. This trailed for some 3 feet behind her as she walked, and was exactly the same sort of thing that the leader of a patrol of aeroplanes uses so that he can be identified.

When the "Baron" returned to the farmyard everything else there immediately concentrated its attention upon the weird sight. Chickens, ducks, pigs, and geese all followed the big sow as she walked around. It was certainly a successful circus for our friend von Richthofen, and every time she moved around that farmyard she had a good following of multi-coloured admirers.

Upon the express condition that we would not paint them, the farmer let us have his rabbits in the afternoon. He must have had over 200, and we would go in with a blanket and get about twenty-five small ones, then take them out and drop them in the green grass, where we would sit around under a tree, and play with them or watch them eat. They were amusing little things and passed away many hours for us.

However, dogs were our special favourites, so far as pets were concerned, and every stray dog we could find we would pick up and bring home. Finally we had a huge collection of them, with a variety of names ranging from "Kate," "Rachel," or "Horace" to "Black Dog" and "Nigger."

They were all good dogs, and I remember well when little Kate, whom we had raised from a puppy, was lost.

We all felt very badly for days. She was reported in the squadron books as "missing," as she had gone out and had not returned. Poor Kate! her life had indeed been hard. As a puppy, her first accident was when she had "crashed" off the top of a piano, and had broken one of her fore legs. This was no sooner mended than somebody walked on her when she was sitting in front of the fire, and broke another. A month later an automobile ran over her on the road, and broke a third and badly injured her body, so that she was a little cripple, and hopped along on three legs, although how she ever used them nobody knows. Her body was all twisted, and she had no good points except a very charming manner, which made us very fond of her.

"Nigger" was one of my own dogs. One night, returning after having dined with some other unit, I found "Nigger" outside my hut. He was a big dog, looking very much like an Airedale, only black. It was pouring rain and very cold, so I took him in and let him sleep on my bed with me. He had a most affectionate way about him, and although quite the smelliest dog I have ever known, it was a pleasure to have him about.

The other dogs each had their good points. Rachel—who was a little deformed fox-terrier we had picked up on the road simply because she was the ugliest-looking thing we had ever seen—turned out to be a wonderful ratter, frequently taking on rats twice as long as she was, and, although getting badly bitten herself, she would invariably come out of the scrap victorious. Nobody would claim Rachel, but she got fed somehow, and also got quite a lot of attention, so she stayed with us.

By way of sports, we played tennis a great deal, and did considerable riding, two good horses having been lent to the squadron for that purpose. Then, too, as the place seemed to be infested with rats, we managed to get together some good ratting parties, and with the help of some of the dogs had many successful hunts.

Carefully blocking all the holes in the ground, with the exception of one or two, we would send smoke down one of these, and with a little preliminary squeal three or four rats would rush out of the other. One afternoon, inside of half an hour, we caught eighteen rats.

Another sport, and a very good one, was to take a 22-calibre rifle and try to shoot individual pigeons on the wing. It was a very hard thing to do and required much practise. Luckily we did not hit too often, as we paid well for each pigeon we shot down. I remember one afternoon firing 500 rounds and only hitting one pigeon, and I considered myself lucky to hit that one. This sport was much encouraged, as it was the very best practise in the world for the eye of a man whose business it is to fight mechanical birds in the air.

Every now and again we would be given a day off. This day would be spent, usually, in either sleeping all day or roaming about the orchard in silk pyjamas, or else one would go and visit some friends who possibly were stationed near. It was a great thing, as it always left us keen for work the next day.

CHAPTER 17

BY THIS TIME I had learned nearly all of the fundamental principles of fighting in the air and had more or less decided upon exactly what tactics were best for me to use. I also realized the exact limit of my ability in carrying these various tactics out, and in fighting acted accordingly. I was more than ever firmly resolved now that, having got so far in the game and past its most dangerous stages, I would take no foolish risks, but continue to wait for the best opportunities. It was very hard to restrain oneself at times, but from the middle of May until I left France in August, I lost only one man out of my patrol killed, and he was shot down on an expedition when I was not with him.

When flying alone, on a day off or something like that, I took queer chances, it is true, but flying with the patrol often let opportunities slip by because they were not quite good enough; but when the right ones came, we were quick to seize them and were nearly always successful.

I had learned that the most important thing in fighting was the shooting, next the various tactics in coming into the fight, and last of all flying ability itself. The shooting, as I have said before, I practised constantly and became more and more expert at it, with the result that finally I had great confidence in myself, and knew for a certainty that if I only could get in a shot from one or two of my favourite positions, I would be successful in downing my opponent.

To those who have never seen a war machine I would explain that to control one, the pilot has to manipulate but a single lever which we call the "joy-stick." It is very much like the lever with which you shift gears on an automobile, but it moves in four directions. If you want your machine to go down, the instinctive move would be to lean the body forward. Therefore, the fighting aeroplane is so rigged that when the pilot pushes the "joy-stick" forward, the nose of the machine points down. In the same way, if he pulls the "joy-stick" back, the nose goes up and the machine climbs at any angle he wants it to. In turning, it is necessary to bank the machine, otherwise it will skid outwards. It is also just as necessary that the machine is not banked too much. This is one of the first things a pupil is taught when learning to fly.

The "joy-stick" also controls the banking. By moving it to either side you can tilt up whichever wing is desired. At his feet the pilot has a rudder bar which controls the horizontal direction of the machine. If he pushes his left foot forward and banks slightly, the machine turns slowly to the left. To go to the right, there is only necessary a push with the right foot and a slight bank. The pilot thus has both feet on the rudder bar, holds the "joy-stick" with his right hand, and with his left controls the engine of the machine by holding the throttle in his hand. He is always able to do anything he wishes, either with the engine or the machine itself. When firing the gun, he simply moves his thumb slightly along the "joy-stick" and presses the lever which pulls the trigger.

176

To be able to fight well, a pilot must be able to have absolute control over his machine. He must know by the "feel" of it exactly how the machine is, what position it is in, and how it is flying, so that he may manœuvre rapidly, and at the same time watch his opponent or opponents. He must be able to loop, turn his machine over on its back, and do various other flying "stunts"— not that these are actually necessary during a combat, but from the fact that he has done these things several times he gets absolute confidence, and when the fight comes along he is not worrying about how the machine will act. He can devote all his time to fighting the other fellow, the flying part of it coming instinctively. Thus the flying part, although perhaps the hardest to train a man for, is the least important factor in aerial fighting. A man's flying ability may be perfect. He may be able to control the machine and handle it like no one else on earth, but if he goes into a fight and risks his life many times to get into the right position for a good shot, and then upon arriving there cannot hit the mark, he is useless. Unable to shoot his opponent down, he must risk his life still more in order to get out and away from the enemy, and that is why I put aerial gunnery down as the most important factor in fighting in the air.

Tactics are next important because, by the proper use of the best tactics, it is so easy to help eliminate risks and also so easy to put the enemy at a great disadvantage. Surprise is always to be aimed for. Naturally if one can surprise the enemy and get into a proper position to shoot before he is aware of your presence, it simplifies matters tremendously, and there should be no second part to the

177

fight. But it is a very hard thing to do, as every fighting man in the air is constantly on the look-out for enemy machines. To surprise him requires a tremendous amount of patience and many failures before one is ever successful. A point to know is the fact that it is easier to surprise a formation of four or six than it is to surprise one or two. This is probably because the greater number feel more confident in their ability to protect themselves, and also are probably counting upon each other to do a certain amount of the looking out.

When flying alone or with just one other, it is always a case of constantly turning around in your seat, turning your machine to right or left, looking above and around or below you all the time. It is a very tiring piece of work, so it is but natural that when you have three or four other men behind you, you spend more time looking in the direction where you hope the enemy machines are, if you want to attack them, and to looking at any interesting sights which are on the ground.

In ordinary fight or duel we had tactics, of course, to suit the occasion. The great thing is never to let the enemy's machine get behind you, or "on your tail." Once he reaches there it is very hard to get him off, as every turn and every move you make, he makes with you. By the same token it is exactly the position into which you wish to get, and once there you must constantly strive for a shot as well as look out for attacks from other machines that may be near. It is well if you are against odds never to stay long after one machine. If you concentrate on him for more than a fraction of a second, some other Hun has a chance to get a steady shot at you, without taking any risks himself. To hit a machine when it is flying at right angles to you across your nose is very hard. It requires a good deal of judgment in knowing just how far ahead of him to aim. It is necessary to hit the pilot himself and not the machine to be successful, and also necessary to hit the pilot in the upper part of the body where it will be more certain to put him completely out of action at once. When a machine goes into flames it is largely a matter of luck, as it means that several of your bullets have pierced the petrol tank and ignited the vapour escaping from it.

In our tactics we used this cross shot, as it is called, considerably; mainly when, after a combat has been broken off for some reason, guns having jammed or the engine running badly, it becomes necessary to escape. Upon turning to flee, your opponent is able to get a direct shot at you from behind. This is decidedly dangerous; so, watching carefully over your shoulder and judging the moment he will open fire, you turn your machine quickly so as to fly at right angles to him. His bullets will generally pass behind you during the manoeuvre. The next thing to do is to turn facing him and open with your cross fire.

In fighting in company with other machines of your own squadron one must be very careful to avoid collisions, and it is also necessary to watch all of them carefully as well as the enemy, because it is a code of honour to help out any comrade who is in distress, and no matter how serious the consequences may seem, there is only one thing to do— dash straight in, and at least lend moral support to him. In one case I had a Captain out of my own squadron, a New Zealander, come eight miles across the lines after both his guns had choked, and he was entirely useless as a fighting unit, just to try to bluff away seven of the enemy who were attacking me. It was unnecessary in this case, as I had the upper hand of the few machines that were really serious about the fight; but it was a tremendously brave act on his part, as he ran great risks of being killed, while absolutely helpless to defend himself in any way.

All fights vary slightly in the tactics required, and it is necessary to think quickly and act instantly. Where a large number of machines are engaged, one great thing is always to be the upper man—that is, to be slightly higher than your particular opponent. With this extra height it is quite easy to dive upon him, and it makes manœuvring much easier. If, as is often the case, you are the "under dog," it is a very difficult position, and requires great care to carry on the fight with any chance of success. Every time your opponent attempts to dive at you or attack you in any way, the best thing to do is to turn on him, pull the nose of your machine up, and fire. Often while fighting it is necessary to attack a machine head-on until you seem to be just about to crash in mid-air. Neither machine wants to give way, and collisions have been known to occur while doing this. We prided ourselves that we hardly ever gave way, and the German was usually the first to swerve. At the last moment one of you must dodge up and the other down, and there is great risk of both of you doing the same thing, which of course is fatal. It is perhaps one of the most thrilling moments in fighting in the air when you are only 100 yards apart, and coming together at colossal speed, spouting bullets at each other as fast as you can.

Once you have passed you must turn instantly to keep your opponent from getting a favourable position behind you, and then carry on the fight in the usual series of turns and manœuvres. An extraordinary feature of these fights which occupied any length of time, and entailed such manœuvring, was the fact that they were generally undecisive, one machine or the other finally deciding that for some reason or other it must quit and make good its escape. In nearly all cases where machines have been downed, it was during a fight which had been very short, and the successful burst of fire had occurred within the space of a minute after the beginning of actual hostilities.

CHAPTER 18

A NEW KIND OF ENEMY was meeting us now—a two-seater machine which mounted a small cannon, or shell-firing gun. This was a sort of "pom-pom" gun, discharging about a one-pound shell, which would either burst upon percussion or after travelling a certain distance through the air. Several times, while attacking machines doing artillery work, we were surprised to see little white puffs around us, and realized suddenly that these were small bursting shells. However, they did no harm that I know of, and the Huns did not seem to be able to make even decent shooting with them. The first two or three times we met up with them they rather frightened us, and we kept away from their field of fire, but after a little bit of experience we found there was nothing to worry about. Their shooting was so bad the shells invariably burst well to one side. Personally, I much preferred "pom-pom" to the wicked rattle of a pair of machine guns pointing at me and their smoking bullets whining by.

Day after day we chased these machines away from their work, only to have to go out an hour later and chase them again. Sometimes we would force them right down to the ground, and that would often finish them for the day, but it was very seldom that anything decisive occurred.

On June 24th in the early morning, while leading a patrol, I ran into a German pilot of exceptional quality. Another fighting patrol of ours had been attacking him, when I saw him, and I headed in their direction to watch the fight, but they evidently had had enough of it, and left him. We, in our turn, took him on, and there followed an extremely hot engagement. He managed to get into the middle of us, and it was all we could do to keep from colliding as we attacked him. Finally, to add to our disgust, he broke off the combat of his own sweet will just at the moment he felt he had had enough, and dived away. As we followed, diving after him, he would turn under us, then dive again, and repeat this performance. It was a most trying thing. I would dive after him, then the moment I stopped firing and pulled up to turn and watch where he went, I would probably just miss by inches one of our own machines, also diving at him, with his eyes on nothing but the enemy. The danger of collision in such an attack is very great, and requires a constant look-out.

Later in the morning I went out again, alone, and saw two enemy scouts. I climbed up above them, and watched carefully, deciding that I would take no chances of losing them. Finally, I discovered that they were patrolling a given beat, and by waiting up above, at one end of this beat, I was able, just at the moment that they turned to go back along it again, to dive down, approaching them from behind, and come up behind the rear one without him seeing me. I got within 20 yards of him, and, just slightly underneath and behind, I pulled the nose of my machine up and with very careful aim opened fire. A second later and his machine smoked a bit, then suddenly burst into flames and fell toward the ground. The other one had dived away from me at first, but now climbed back to attack me. I dived at him twice, and opened fire both times, but without result. The second time I think he was hit, but not seriously, as he dived away and escaped, going through the clouds.

Not long after that I met three more of the enemy, and had a funny fight with them, by worrying them from above. In the course of a number of short dives I suddenly ran out of ammunition. They had seemed, up to this moment, quite keen to fight, and so was I, but now I decided I must get away somehow. I was somewhat surprised when I discovered that at the same moment I commenced to escape, they also did. We both noticed at the same time that the other side was willing to break it off, and as the Hun turned to attack me behind, while I was escaping, I turned to try to bluff him away. It worked perfectly, and the whole three of them again turned their noses east and flew away. It had been some time since I had brought down an enemy machine, and I hoped the one in flames this day would change my luck for the better again. I think it did, for in the week which followed I brought down five in all.

Victory flew with me the following day when I managed to get two more scouts on my list. While flying alone, I saw three of them protecting a two-seater. They were very intent upon watching their charge and had not noticed me, so I flew away some distance and climbed well above them, to make certain they had no machines in layer formation above. Then I dived on the three scouts. Again I surprised the rear man, and after twenty-five rounds, well placed, he burst into flames and went down. The other two were at the moment turning toward me; but upon seeing the fate of their comrade, one of them dived away and went down near the two-seater. The other one turned to engage me. In the short fight that followed, he got some bullets very close to me, and I to him, but for three or four minutes neither of us seemed able to get an appreciable advantage of the other. Then, suddenly I managed to get a chance from an angle I knew very well, and opened fire. He immediately dropped out of control, and I dived after him, firing as he fell. Having finished one drum of ammunition, I had to come out of the dive to put a new one on. The other scout and two-seater were still in the same place, so getting above them I tried two dives, but without result. The observer on the two-seater was doing remarkably good shooting, and I did not like to get too close, as it seemed a poor way to end a morning's work by being shot down after starting so well. Finishing my ammunition at fairly long range, I returned home.

My luck still held the next day when I found some more scouts, in straggling formation. The rear one was slightly above the rest, which was very much to my liking, so down I went after him. Again the surprise was successful, and, after a short burst, out of control he went. I was getting quite callous in doing this, and was afraid of myself becoming careless. The only danger I ran was in the fact that I might become careless, and if caught while creeping up behind these people, and they had a chance to turn on me, it would be a very unhappy position to be in. However, this time it was as successful as the rest, and as two more scouts who were next highest seemed willing to fight, I went down after them. As I approached, one of the two lost his nerve and dived away. The other made a turn to come at me, but I opened fire, with rough aim, while still a hundred yards

186

away. It was a purely lucky shot, and one of my bullets must have accidentally hit an important wire in his machine, as suddenly, while doing an exceedingly quick turn, two of his planes flew away and his machine fell in pieces.

I did not have any more luck for several days, most of my fights being in the usual job of chasing away artillery machines—taking all the risks, and never having a chance to get in a decent shot.

A few days later, while out in the morning, thick clouds prevented our seeing very much. Several times, while going around or under the clouds, I would suddenly catch sight of an enemy machine, then lose it again a moment or two later. Once I saw a scout about 300 yards away, but he immediately dived toward some clouds, and I could only open fire from long range in the hope of frightening him down. Meeting up with one of my own squadron, who was also flying alone, a few minutes later, we discovered a machine directly underneath us. Down we both went at him, and opened fire, but he also disappeared into a cloud, and we flew away. Five minutes later he again appeared beneath us. Down at him we went, but again he dug himself into the clouds.

After each fight it would be necessary to make certain where you were, as a strong wind from the west kept blowing the machines in toward Hunland. I had five fights in the course of the morning, but none of them was successful or very exciting.

The next day at noon, however, I had enough excitement to last me for some time. While on patrol and flying nearly three miles up, I saw approaching us from the direction of Germany a fast Hun two-seater of the enemy. I guessed at once he thought to cross our lines, and flew to attack him. He had seen us, however, and headed in the other direction immediately. I found I could not catch up with him, so, in great disgust, gave up the chase; then, on thinking it over, decided that if he had orders to cross the lines he would probably make another attempt. So I flew well off to one side and climbed as fast as I could. I could just see him— a speck in the distance—and could see that he also was climbing. Finally, when he reached what he surmised was a safe height he approached our lines again. I did not make another attempt to stop him, hoping that he would get well across, and then I would come between him and his own country. He saw me attempt to do this, and evidently hoped to evade me by climbing up still higher. A height of eighteen thousand feet was reached, and we were still climbing at about the same pace. He went well into our territory, and I followed at a great distance, watching carefully; then, the moment he started for home, went after him. At 19,500 feet we approached each other. I opened fire while coming head-on at him. He swerved slightly, and in doing so upset my aim. If we had been lower, I could certainly have hit him, but the great height and great cold had made my hand numb and a little unsteady in controlling the machine. He flew across, in front of me, and I turned with him to get in another shot. His observer's face I could make out, as he was firing his gun frantically at me. We passed only about 10 yards apart, yet I was shooting so badly I did not bring him down. Then, in holding the nose of my machine up, to get a last shot at him, I lost too much speed, and suddenly fell several thousand feet completely out of control. By the time I had straightened out the enemy had escaped, and, in disgust, I rejoined the rest of the patrol and continued to fly up and down the lines.

Just as we intended returning, I saw five of the enemy some distance away, and underneath us, so flew over and engaged them from above. The fight was at 7000 feet, the height I liked the best, so I went into it vigorously. Suddenly, while diving on a Hun machine, I heard the rattle of a pair of machine guns just behind me. I was certain that I had been trapped and was being fired at from a few feet behind me, so turned quickly, just to see one of our own machines shoot by underneath me. I continued my dive again, but the opportunity was lost, so went down after another one of the machines. For ten minutes this fight continued. Many times I would dive down, open fire, and then come up and turn away, at the same time avoiding others of our machines which were diving and firing as they came. At last I was successful. One of the Germans seemed to be enjoying the fight and had the impudence to loop directly under me. I happened to be diving just as he reached the top of the loop, and as he was coming out of it I got a direct shot on to the bottom of his machine, as it was turned upside-down. He fell out of control and crashed on the ground underneath us.

Another machine had now joined the fight—a machine from one of our naval squadrons stationed in France—and he also was doing very well, as I saw a machine which he fired at fall out of control. Then suddenly, the remainder of the Germans—they had been reinforced by others—turned away and escaped, flying very near the ground. We returned home, and I waved to our new acquaintance from the naval squadron, so he followed me back to the aerodrome and landed beside me, to tell me that he had also seen my machine crash. It turned out that this man was the one who was leading the naval flyers and was next to me, at that time, in the number of machines which had been brought down by an Englishman then in France. It was his twenty-fifth machine.

CHAPTER 19

WE WERE GREATLY EXCITED now over the fact that in a few weeks we expected to have a new type of machine— a much faster and better one all round. It also had two guns instead of one, which made a great difference; so night and day we dreamt and thought of these new machines and the time we would have when they arrived.

The next week was a quiet one, only a few Huns were being seen, and the engagements we had were short ones, at long ranges. But on the evening of July 10th we had a most interesting time. The day had been very cloudy, and there had been no flying. In the afternoon two of us went off in a car to pick up some friends and bring them back to the aerodrome in the evening. This was the day that Rachel was first found and brought to be a member of our squadron. My flight was detailed for a job at 7 o'clock that evening; but when that time arrived, the clouds were so low we decided it would not be worth while going up, so all roamed down to the tennis-court. The weather became a bit clearer when we had finished three or four games of a set. It was part of a tournament we were playing, and quite an interesting game was on when suddenly a messenger came down with the news that six machines were to leave the ground. We all ran to our machines. We were still in our white flannels, and dressed more for comfort than a fight in the air. There was no time to change, however, so into the machines we crawled and started aloft. The Major, deciding there must be some excitement in the air, otherwise we would not have been sent out, decided to follow us.

Twenty minutes after we had been told on the tennis-court that a job was on hand, we sighted some Huns flying slightly above us. It was now a wonderful evening, everything clear as crystal, and one could not but feel that such a thing as a German should not be allowed in the sky, to spoil the beauty of the dying day. So, regardless of position or tactics of any kind, I led straight into the German formation. They were evidently a new squadron on that part of the front. They were flying machines of a bright green— machines which I had never seen before. However, they were no more courageous than most of their comrades, and when they saw us coming, although they had every advantage, they turned to go the other way. We cut them off, and managed to come in partly underneath them. There were twelve of them and seven of us, counting the Major, who had followed us into the fight, and a merry mix-up began at once. Several times I became entirely separated from the rest, and was in a very dangerous position. Once, after chasing one of the Huns for a moment, I turned, to find another one coming down directly at me, so I pulled up my nose to fire straight at him. The same moment a third Hun came diving at me from the side. He had an excellent shot, and knowing I could not shoot at him at the moment, on he came. I felt I was certainly in a very tight corner, when suddenly, with a flash of silver above me and the rattle of a machine gun, I saw my Major's machine go dead at the German. It was a wonderful sight. The Hun quickly turned away, and at the same time the other man who was attacking me turned also. I then lost sight of the Major, but continued in the whirlwind of the fight. Round and round each other the whole lot of us went, like a lot of sparrows in a great whirlwind. Suddenly one of the Germans appeared just in front of me, and I opened fire dead at him. Down he went out of control, and I turned to engage some more, but after a few minutes they all dived away.

The people at home on the aerodrome were now having a most exciting time. A little over half an hour after the patrol had left the ground they saw a silver Nieuport come streaking home. It landed, and they could see by the number that it was the Major's machine. They went up to him, and he quietly crawled out and spoke to the people around him, saying that there was a big fight on over the lines, and we were all in the middle of it. He then turned and walked to the office, where he telephoned to report that he had been in a fight. Then, sending for the medical orderly, informed him he had a "scratch."

The medical orderly almost fainted when he saw blood pouring down the Major's sleeve. It turned out that when he had been diving to save me, a chance bullet from one of the Huns, who was sitting safely at the edge of the fight, had struck his machine, actually hitting the switch, where it exploded, one fragment of it entering his forearm and going right up above the elbow. It made a very nasty wound indeed. The bullet, as well as smashing the switch and his arm, had done other damage, destroying several instruments and breaking an oil-indicator. The moment he realized that he had been hit, the Major carefully set about with his other arm to turn off the oil and adjust the switch, so that it would work properly. It was a delicate job, and all the time he was bleeding freely. Then it was necessary to get clear of the fight. This, of course, is a difficult thing to do at the best of times, but in a case like the Major's it would have seemed almost impossible. Luck, however, favoured him, for at just that moment a chance came, and he took it. He slipped away toward our lines, and losing height, came toward home. The next thing he feared was the fact that he might faint in the air from loss of blood, so, terrified of this, he held his arm over the side in the cold air, and that partially stopped the bleeding. He then came down and landed.

As I have said, the people at home were having a most exciting time. The sudden leaving of the rest of us for a job over the lines had been quite a dramatic affair, and now, as they sat on the ground, first appeared one of the machines, back in half an hour, with its pilot wounded, then not a sign of the rest for what seemed a very long time. They wondered if we had all been shot down, or what in the world could have happened. However, in an hour and a half the rest of us were back. We had been looking carefully, in the hope that we would find some more of the enemy, but had only seen two of them, which we were unable to catch up with. We did not know what had happened to the Major until we landed, by which time he had gone to the hospital. Four days later we were all pleased to see him back on the job again, although, of course, unable to fly. He had been operated on, but to lie in bed in a hospital was agony for him, so, slipping away, he managed to get back to the aerodrome, where he stayed. A few weeks later, unfortunately for us, he was promoted to the rank of colonel, and left. The squadron felt very badly at his loss for some time, and only the fact that the man who took his place was also of the same calibre ever reconciled us to it at all.

The Huns seemed now to be concentrating a lot of flying in the evenings. Every evening, when we went out, we were certain of a fight, and usually a long fight, sometimes lasting as long as half an hour, and on one occasion lasting for three-quarters of an hour. These fights were always referred to as "dog fights," as it nearly always meant just dashing in, then out again and in again, and never really doing any harm, yet always in a terrible sort of mix-up.

On July 12th I was successful in coming up behind some Huns and managed to get another one down—crashed. Then, for several days, I had no more luck, although combats were numerous. On one occasion I was nearly caught in a bad trap, when, on following a machine, I suddenly saw about twenty more trying to close in around me. I left off the chase, and got out just in time.

Almost every evening we would find well-laid traps set for us, and it required careful manœuvring and tactics to avoid falling into them. Several times, indeed, we did, and it took a lot of trouble to get out safely. Four or five Huns would come along, and we would engage them; then, while having a "dog fight," suddenly as many as fifteen to twenty more would appear from all angles and join in the fight. This thing happened every day, and the Huns were evidently out to get us. They were devoting every energy to it, and if the men in the air had been as determined as the people on the ground who ordered them to go out, we would have had a more difficult time of it.

One evening, while out, I managed to surprise a Hun, and got within 15 feet of his tail plane before I opened fire. Just a few shots, and he burst into flames, and fell. His companion did not stay, and managed to escape from me, diving vertically toward the ground. I shoved the nose of my machine down until it was pointing vertically as well, opening fire on him as the two of us dived; but his was a heavier machine than mine, and it fell faster, so he rapidly increased the distance between us, with the result that I was left behind. Coming out of my dive, I headed in a homeward direction. On the way, I saw a large "dog fight" going on, as many as twenty-five machines being engaged in it. I flew over to the mêlée as fast as I could reach it, afraid as usual that it would be over before I could get there; but luck was with me, as I managed to catch, on the edge of the fight, an enemy who was trying to attack one of our machines. He did not see me, and was flying straight away, so the shot was an easy one and could not be missed. I opened fire, and he fell out of control. Then, unable to watch him down, I went on to the other combats. Later, some of the other people reported they had seen him strike the earth, crash, and burst into flames; so there was not much doubt as to his fate.

This "dog fight" lasted for twenty minutes after I had joined it. Several times the only intimation I had that anyone was firing on me would be the streaks of smoke as some bullets had passed near by. Sometimes the shooting would be so bad it would be over a hundred yards away; at other times within ten feet of me. But owing to the rapid way in which one manœuvres during such a fight, it was a very difficult thing to hit a man. The excitement of the fight, and the fact that it is necessary to watch all the time to avoid colliding with your friends, does not give one time to think of the danger of being hit, and, to tell the truth, you do not realize that these little streaks of smoke which go by you are really deadly bullets.

The next day, while out, I tried to surprise three of the enemy, but failed, and found it necessary to engage the top one. I was slightly under him, and it was a difficult proposition. However, I managed to get as close as 50 yards and opened fire. The other two were now so near me that I felt it unhealthy to concentrate my attention altogether on one. For a few minutes, then, I had it rather warm. Every time one would begin to fire at me, I would switch the nose of my machine in his direction and fire a few bullets at random. This would make him turn away for a second. Then I would switch it to another. Suddenly an opportunity for escape presented itself. I took it as quickly as it came, and managed to get clean away. I then flew higher, and later found two more of the enemy, flying together. Again I decided to try a surprise, and this time was successful. Thirty yards away I got my sights well in line with a point on the enemy machine which would mean that I was going to hit the pilot, and I pulled the trigger. A moment later his machine side-slipped, turned completely over on its back, and then went down. Anxious to make it a double success, I turned to catch his comrade, but he had decided to escape, and was 300 yards away. I fired a few shots at him, just to hurry him up, and then turned to watch the machine I had brought down. It was still falling out of control, and away below me I saw it tumbling like a piece of paper thrown from a high window. Eventually it disappeared through the clouds.

I did not have any feeling of compunction in cases like this. The idea of killing was, of course, always against my nature, but for two reasons I did not mind it: one, and the greater one, of course, being that it was another Hun down, and so much more good done in the war; secondly, it was paying back some of the debts I owed the Huns for robbing me of the best friends possible. Then, too, in the air one did not altogether feel the human side of it. As I have said before, it was not like killing a man so much as just bringing down a bird in sport.

In going into a fight now, I felt none of those thrills which I used to feel at first. I was quite cool and collected, but probably did not enjoy it as much as I did in the days when a certain amount of anxiety and fear was felt just before the fight started. But the moment my machine gun commenced to fire, I felt the old feeling of exultation, and this always remained with me throughout the whole of every fight I have had.

CHAPTER 20

THE NEW MACHINES were almost ready now and at any time we were to use them, but in the meantime I was working hard with my Nieuport. One day at noon, while out alone, I came as near being brought down as it was possible to be. There were very few machines in the sky, and about a thousand feet above some clouds I saw three of the Huns. If I had followed my old tactics, I would have carefully gone far away and climbed to high above them, then come down from that direction; but I suppose "familiarity breeds contempt," and I imagine I was getting a little careless. Anyway, I had not the patience this time to waste all of those minutes, so I climbed straight up at them. It meant that I was going much slower than I would otherwise have been, with the dive. They were out of a squadron—I could tell by their markings—that I had often before attacked, and probably before I had seen them they had seen me.

They let me come on up underneath them, knowing that I would not fire until I was at very close range. Then, when I was about 100 yards away and some 100 feet below, the whole three of them turned on me. I did not even have time to attempt an escape; the whole three were diving at me at once, all firing. It was an awkward moment, so I pulled my machine back and fired straight at one of them; then, switching quickly, I gave a burst to another. By this time the third was down to my level; so, turning, I faced him and opened fire. He "zoomed" up and reached several hundred feet above me, from where he dived again. It was a terrible moment, and I could not think how to escape, as they had the most favourable positions from which to attack me, and no danger of anybody worrying them while they were doing it.

Then suddenly I realized that the clouds were only a thousand feet below me, and even less by this time, as I had been losing height, so with a kick of my rudder I threw my machine suddenly out of control, and let it stay out of control until I was enveloped in a soft, white, fleecy cloud. Here I knew that it was hopeless to try to regain control, so I waited. I must have gone through the clouds for over a thousand feet—it seemed years and years. I was terrified that it might be a thick, thick cloud, all the way down to the ground. However, suddenly I saw things appearing, and underneath me was the ground. I was in a spinning nose-dive, but it was easy to recover control, and I flattened away and flew straight back to the aerodrome. It was a lesson to me, and, strange to say, the last occasion upon which I had a good opportunity to try that stunt, as a few days later we went on to the new machines.

When our first job on the new machines came, it was a great moment for me. I felt that at last the time had arrived when I could really do some good work, so went after it with my heart altogether on it.

On our first job we were told we must not cross the lines—only just stay on them, and chase anything away. You can imagine how pleased I was, after carefully getting up to the required height, and feeling this wonderful, new, high-powered machine under me, suddenly to see an enemy machine on our side. I gave chase, but it slipped across the lines when I was only a half a mile away. I was very much annoyed to be unable to follow it.

To get on these new machines, after the old ones, made one feel that all you had to do was to open fire on any old enemy at all—just get near enough to him to do that—and he was bound to be yours. As a matter of fact it was almost that easy, and the strenuous days of fighting that I had experienced on a Nieuport were really gone. The new job was much less of work and much more of pleasure.

Then my disgust was great when the weather became bad, and stayed that way for three days. However, by this time I had been able to get my machine into better order, and was keener for a fight than I had ever been before.

I went out alone as soon as the weather was fit, and after patrolling over the enemy territory for several hours I saw one two-seater at a tremendous height. I could not get quite up to him, but when a thousand feet underneath, I pulled my machine back until it pointed straight up, and fired that way. I did this twice, but both times failed to do any damage. We had then reached so far into enemy territory that I thought it advisable to return home, so turned and came back. The anti-aircraft fire seemed to be absolutely nothing to worry about, compared to what it had been in the slower machine. We were twenty-five miles an hour faster, and it made a great difference. The shells seemed all to burst behind me, and far away. I felt that all the risk had gone, and that I was now in for a really good time in France.

On the 28th of the month I went out in the evening

to do a patrol, just on the German side of the lines. Faithfully I stayed at this place for over an hour, but then it became more than I could stand, as there was not a German machine in sight. I decided to take a look in Hunland. I flew about fifteen miles in before I saw a single German, and then, well off to one side, there were three of them. I did not care whether they had seen me or not; all I wanted to do was to get right into the middle of them and mix it up, so I came straight at them. They had seen me, however, and one, detaching himself from the rest, came in my direction. He came straight at me, and we approached head-on, both of us with our engines in front, and both firing two guns. I could see his bullets streaking by about 5 feet to the left of me, and mine, as I watched them through my sights, seemed to be making better shooting. He suddenly swerved, but I managed to get into a favourable position behind him in the course of one or two turns, and again opened fire. This time I was altogether successful, as his machine suddenly burst into flames. The others had kept well away, and were now escaping as fast as they could. I did my best to catch one up, and if we had only been a little higher would have done so, but I felt I was getting too close to the ground that distance behind the lines, so opening fire from long range, I shot away about 100 rounds, then turned and headed toward home. It was my first Hun shot down in this new type of machine, and the first in the squadron.

Late one evening I went out again in a Nieuport, and got mixed up in a bad "dog fight." It lasted for three-quarters of an hour, and during that whole time I don't think fifteen seconds went by that I did not have to turn my machine sharply in one direction or another, or do some other manœuvre.

While engaging a few machines at the top of the fight, I saw underneath me a Nieuport, evidently in difficulty in the middle of a lot of Huns, so with one other of my squadron I started down to him, fighting all the way and striving for nothing but to frighten the Huns off, in order that we could get there in time to help our man. He seemed to be fighting very well, as his machine was turning around to the left, banking vertically, and turning very quickly. At 12,000 feet we started this, but by the time we had reached him he was 500 feet from the ground. I had long ago wondered what was the matter, as he was going down almost as fast as we could come down to him. I could not understand why he did not see us, and in some way realize that if he stayed there a moment we would be down to help him; but instead his machine kept turning, doing a left-hand spiral, and going down rapidly. At 1000 feet from him we managed to frighten away the two Huns, who were both engaging him. Then, turning to clear the fight, I looked over my shoulder to see if he was following; but no—he was still in the spiral. I was afraid, for the moment, that he thought I was another Hun, so went off to one side for a bit, but he continued spiralling, and realizing that something was very wrong, I flew back toward him.

Just at that moment his machine spiralled straight into the ground, a few hundred feet underneath me. I made two or three turns over the spot, regardless of the fight above me, to determine whether or not he had been badly hurt, but could not see. I expected, every moment, some

203

people to come running up and work at the smashed machine to get him out, but there was no sign of anybody moving. The other Nieuport that had come down with me was lower than I was, and the idea seemed to come to both of us, as the country appeared smooth enough, to land and see what was wrong. We both thought we were well this side of our own lines, as the trenches could be seen about three-quarters of a mile to the east of us. Picking out a smooth piece of ground just near the smashed machine, I came down to glide on to it. Then, hearing the crackle of rifles and machine guns around, I put my engine on again and turned away, cursing the people on the ground for firing at me, thinking all the time it was our own troops making a mistake. I had now come down to a height of several hundred feet, and suddenly saw German uniforms in a small hollow in the ground underneath me. It was a narrow escape, as both of us might have landed there and quietly been taken prisoners, without ever having a chance to escape.

A few days later I learned that in this particular place the people holding the line were not in trenches, but in outposts, practically in the open field, and the line of trenches behind them was the Hindenburg line, where the Germans evidently intended retreating, when necessary.

Almost every one of my fights in the new machine were successful. Three of us went out early one Sunday morning, when the sun, shining from the east on a thick ground-mist, made it very difficult to see. Clouds were also in the sky, making it impossible to go above 7000 feet. Our new type of machines were evidently greatly feared by the Germans, as the moment we approached the lines, two

two-seaters of the enemy, while just specks in the distance, were obviously signalled to from the ground, for they immediately dived straight down and did not return. This happened again fifteen minutes later, when we sighted another of the artillery machines. They were terrified of this type, and would not stay to fight us.

Then suddenly I saw four enemy scouts, and at the same moment they saw us. They approached, obviously with the intention of attacking us, but when only 300 yards away recognized the machines we were flying, and turned away quickly. They had been looking for easier prey, and were not very anxious for battle. We went after them, though, and owing to our superior speed were able to catch up with them. Into the middle of them we went, and there followed a merry scrap. One of our trio, by some misfortune, got mixed up in a bad position, as he was not seen again, and must have been shot down. The other man's guns had both jammed at the beginning of the fight, and he was so furious at this bad luck that for several minutes he stayed in the fight, just to bluff the Huns. Then one of them made it a little nasty for him, and it was necessary to escape. Back to the lines he went, making short dashes of 100 yards every now and then, two Huns following him all the way, and firing at him as he went, but owing to pure good flying and clever manœuvring he was able to avoid even having his machine hit. Then, on looking back from the lines, he saw the fight going on some distance over, and realizing that I was alone in the middle of it he came back all that way, without either of his guns in working order. I referred to this in an earlier part of my book, and I still think it one of the bravest deeds I have ever heard of, as he had a hard time getting back to me, and then also in escaping a second time. He returned to the aerodrome, landed, had his guns fixed, and immediately hastened out again in the hope he would be able to help me.

I, for my part, was having the time of my life. The rattle of my two machine guns was too much for the Huns, altogether. They did not like it at all. I was above the whole lot of them, the original four having been joined by three others now, and they were trying to separate enough so that one or two of their number could get to one side, then climb up and get on top of me. But the moment one of them would begin to go over to one side I would begin to climb, until I would point my nose in his direction, and, flying at wonderful speed, shoot across there, opening fire with rough aim, and down he would dive under the rest. This actually went on for fifteen minutes, during which time another of the enemy came along, and seeing only one British machine in all those Huns, felt safe in attacking me. I opened fire on him with my two guns, and the rattle of them again was sufficient. He did not even return the fire, but dived down and got under the other seven.

After this had gone on about ten minutes, I realized that actually to bring them down I must do better shooting, so picking out the one which was higher than the rest, I concentrated on him and got within 50 yards of him, when I opened fire. He immediately turned over on his back, righted himself, turned over on his back again, and then fell completely out of control. The others I was unable to get, but continued in the fight in the hope that I would be more successful. Out of the corner of my eye I could see a heavy thunderstorm coming up from the direction of the aerodrome. I had to keep my mind on this, as I realized that it was a matter of judging just how long I could keep up the fight before I must make a break for it. At last I decided I had better go, so after a final survey of my "docile children," who seemed to be just sitting under my thumb, I picked out the two or three highest ones and pointed my nose in their direction, on which they dropped down obediently. Then, seizing the opportunity, I dashed away and escaped. They must have been very furious indeed and it must have been bad for the morale of the German infantrymen and gunners on the ground to look up and see one British machine on top of all these Huns, holding them absolutely under his dominion. I reached the aerodrome ten minutes before the thunderstorm broke.

Bad weather then held again for over a week, and it was impossible to fly at all. The evening that it cleared up I was leading my patrol—all of us on the new machines —when I sighted eight of the enemy two miles the other side of the lines. It was just a half-hour before dark, and the light was very bad. I put my engine full on, and headed in their direction. My machine being slightly faster than the remainder of my patrol, I managed to get a bit ahead of them, and carefully picking out the leader of the enemy formation, opened on him. After I had fired about twenty rounds, he turned completely around and headed under me. I turned my sights on to another of his formation, and tried to catch him. Then, over my shoulder, I suddenly saw the machine I had first fired at burst into flames in a most extraordinary way. It happened quite near two of the rest of my patrol, and incidentally rather frightened them, as the machine, which had been smoking slightly, suddenly burst into the whitest flame and fell to the ground, like a ball of livid fire. The man had evidently not been killed, as the machine was not falling out of control, but diving almost vertically toward the ground. Several times, out of the corner of my eye, I glanced at it as it was still falling. Probably it was the bad light that made the flames show so white, but the glare was seen for twenty miles around by people on the ground.

I then made an acquaintance whom I grew to know quite well during the next week or so. It was a silver machine, with small black crosses on it. The pilot had carefully painted his machine, as the silver had been put on to represent the scales of a fish, and covered his planes as well as the body of his machine. During this fight he caused me a lot of worry. Several times I was just able to concentrate on one or two others, when this flying fish would butt in, and force me to a great deal of manœuvring to escape him. Over and over again, while under me, he would pull up his nose and open fire. I would then point my nose down and open back at him, and he would turn away. This was his one weakness—he would not come head-on; so I tried that bluff whenever he began to fire at me.

It was well that I knew this during the fights which followed in the next week. In the middle of this fight both of my guns suddenly jammed, and I could not get them to work. I struggled with them, all the time manœuvring around so that I would not be hit myself. One of the enemy, besides the silver man, had noticed that my guns would not fire, and the two of them came at me and came right up close on one occasion. Just as they did this I managed to get my guns to work, and opened fire, sending the second man down out of control. Old "Silversides," however, had been too wily even to get near the range of my guns, and did nothing but cause me a lot of worry. It was getting dark now, and time to break off the fight, so I decided to escape. Once again the silver fellow came butting in. Every time I would turn toward the lines, he would come at me and open fire. I would dart across his sights, giving him a hard shot, then suddenly turn as if I were going to fire at him. He would turn the nose of his machine away immediately, and I would have a chance again to make a dart for the front. In this way I managed to reach the lines, where he left me. I then returned home, with two more machines to my credit.

The next machine I got was the fortieth aeroplane I had brought down, and, counting my two balloons, my forty-second victory. I had gone out in the morning, about half-past eight, and there did not seem to be many aeroplanes in the sky. I saw a single-seater some distance in toward Germany, and went in after him. He was, however, no picnic. The pilot was one of the very best. Several times we almost got shots at each other, but never a good one. Finally, I opened fire at random, and was greatly surprised to see him go into a spinning dive, but it looked suspicious, and I watched. A little below me he regained control. I dived vertically after him, but was diving too fast, so shot right by him, and he turned away and tried to escape, diving in the opposite direction. I had a second dive after him, but he again went into a spin, even before I had opened fire, and continued spinning straight into the clouds, where I lost him. I had the comfort, however, of knowing that he was not very happy in that spin, as all the time he was going down I was rattling away at him with my guns.

Fifteen minutes later I brought down that fortieth machine. I had seen a two-seater at a tremendous height above me, just a speck in the sky. I was not sure at the moment whether he was British or German, and decided, as there was nothing more interesting, to fly in his direction. He was about two miles our side of the lines, and I imagine now that he was busy taking photographs. When I was about a mile away he saw me, and headed for home. I was still 2000 feet underneath him, and, owing to climbing, was not approaching very fast. However, he did the thing I wished for most of all—he put his nose down to lose height and gain more speed. I was much faster than he was, so I flew level. In a few minutes he had reached my level, and was still losing height. We were now four or five miles inside his own lines, and I was also losing height slightly to gain greater speed. Finally, I managed to get partly into the blind spot underneath his tail, and was rather amused at the observer firing away merrily all the time at me, even when he could hardly see me. I decided to stay there for a minute, in the hope that his gun would jam, or something of that sort happen. Then I proposed to dash in and finish him off at close range. But we travelled on another two miles without anything happening, and had now come down to 6000 feet. It was getting too low for my liking, and we were too far from home, so opening my machine full out I shot in to 75 yards from him, and fired. One burst did the trick, and he began falling in every conceivable sort of way. I rather hoped he would go into flames or fall to pieces, but nothing of that sort occurred, and finally, in a spinning nose-dive, he crashed into a field.

Then I had one of the nastiest times of my life—the return trip home. At 6000 feet I started. Every anti-aircraft gun in the neighbourhood opened fire at me, and they did some wonderful shooting that day. Everywhere I turned there seemed to be huge shells bursting. Several times I heard the little "plank" as they hit my machine in some place, and once quite a large piece struck a plane. I decided that I would lose still more height, in order to come home at a tremendous pace, but in my excitement had forgotten which way the wind was blowing, and have later decided that that was why I was such an easy mark. I was going straight into the teeth of a forty-mile gale, and consequently my speed was much slower than I thought it was. The "Archie" people seemed to have gone mad, or anxious to use up all the ammunition they had in France; anyway, the air was black with bursting shells, and after I had finally reached the lines I looked back, and for five miles could see a path of black smoke from the shells which had been fired at me. They must have fired 500 in all, but luckily I was still intact.

One day, just at this time, I had truly a wonderful surprise. It had been a very rainy day, and as there was no flying I went over to lunch with a cousin of mine, who was stationed only three miles away. After luncheon I returned, and upon seeing my new squadron commander went up to speak to him. He told me that the General in command of the Flying Corps had been trying to get me on the telephone, and said he wanted to speak to me when I came in. I could not imagine why so important a person as the General should want to speak to little "me," but rang him up. My cup of happiness overflowed when he told me that he wanted to be the first to congratulate me upon being awarded the Victoria Cross.

CHAPTER 21

I COULD hardly hold myself down after hearing the great news.

Walking across the aerodrome to the squadron head-quarters, which was stationed on the other side, I had tea with the men there and then came back. The next night we had a big celebration in the way of a dinner, and managed to collect guests who came quite big distances to be there. It was a wonderful success, lasting until after midnight, and several of our guests remained all night and returned early the next morning.

I had a most exciting fight soon after this. The Germans seemed to know my machine, which I had had specially marked with red, white, and blue paint, and in nearly every fight I found that many attemps were made to trap me. Several times I had very narrow escapes in getting away, but always managed at the last moment to squeeze out of it.

It was while flying just under the clouds, I suspected a trap, as the machine with which I was fighting did not seem particularly anxious to come to close quarters, so I pulled my machine back and "zoomed" up through the clouds. The layer was very thin, and I suddenly emerged in the blue sky on the upper side, and just as I did so, I saw the last of a group of German scouts diving vertically. A little to one side there was a huge black burst of

German high explosive. The whole thing was obvious to me at once. The pilot under the clouds had led me to this particular spot, while the people above had been signalled when to dive through to get me.

My revenge was very sweet, because in the heat of the moment, not minding the odds, I dived after them. I came out to find them still diving in front of me, so being not far from one machine, and directly behind it, I opened fire with both guns. It did not need careful shooting; the man went down, never knowing he was hit, continuing his dive straight into the ground. I then pulled up and climbed back into the clouds, and over them, and got away without even a bullet-hole in my machine.

That same afternoon I had several more fights, and ran up against my silver friend again. He was a most persistent rascal, although not very brave in actual fight, and would never leave me alone when I was trying to quit a combat. Several times he followed me right back over our own side of the lines, firing every chance he could get. But even when he was fairly certain my guns were not working, he would not come to close quarters, which, however, was probably lucky for me. He was not a good shot from long range, but the next day he managed to get underneath one of our machines and shot it about quite badly, causing it to return at once and land, seriously damaged.

Several indecisive fights took place about this time, much on the same lines as many others I have described; each one as exciting as the others, but much the same story, both sides ending by breaking off the combats and returning. Several times we lost pilots, and also several times others of the squadron shot down enemy machines.

214

The weather was very bad for some time after this, and although we prayed and prayed for just a few days to get a chance to fight, each morning would find us more restless and worked up because there did not seem to be a chance to get into the air at all.

I was especially keen at this time to fly every moment that was possible, because I had learned a few days before that I would probably be returned to England shortly, for a job there of some sort. I was not at all keen on this, but being a soldier it was not, of course, my opinion that counted, and my work was simply to do as I was told, and to go where I was sent.

One evening I fell into a very nasty trap indeed, just at dusk. I had suddenly seen a single machine of the enemy in front of me, and slightly below. It seemed too good to be true, and I should have known that there was something funny about it; however, down I went on top of him, but somehow missed with my first burst of fire. He dived away a bit and I kept on after him, but by continually diving he kept just out of my reach. This started at 10,000 feet down, and I finally found myself at 2000 feet, and well in the enemy territory. Then, at last, I suspected a trap, and looked about to see what was likely to happen. Sure enough, from above enemy machines were coming down after me, so I turned toward my own lines. There in front of me were twelve more of the Huns. This left nothing to do but turn back and fly farther into enemy territory. This I did, losing height so as to increase my speed. Along I went, with the whole swarm behind. It was lucky for me that my machine was so much faster than theirs. I had to zigzag in my course until I was at least 400 yards in the lead of their first machine, then I flew straight. Dusk was coming on, and I was late and worried as to what to do.

However, there was no advantage in giving in, so I went on as fast as I could tear. I was terrified that I would meet another patrol, but after I had gone about twenty miles due east, I realized the chance for that was very slight, and this comforted me a great deal. But I was still worried as to how I was to get home, as I knew they would wait higher up for me if I climbed. As dusk settled down, I managed to shake off the pack and get completely out of their sight. Then I climbed steadily and turned back toward our own lines. It was light in the upper sky, but quite dark near the ground, and I was at least thirty miles over the German lines. I was never so mad in my life, the annoying part being that such a simple little trick had fooled me into getting into such a nasty position. I had to fly by compass in the approximate direction of home, and just as I reached the lines sighted a lighthouse which I knew, flashing in the dusk. I was happy then and able to land in the last five minutes of light. If I had been just that much later, it would have meant a bad crash landing, for I would have had no idea as to the exact spot where the aerodrome was; but luck was with me still, and I came down without even straining a wire of my machine.

I was disgusted with myself, as it was a bad show, taken all round, and so mad that I did not hand in a report to tell the shameful tale on me.

The day that I learned I was likely to return to England I went out in the evening, and in a very short space of time crammed in a lot of excitement. Flying around beneath the clouds, I had been unable for a time to find anything to fight. There was a complete layer of clouds all over the sky, and this made flying in enemy territory very difficult. The dark sky was such a good background the anti-aircraft guns could pick you out with great accuracy. I forgot about such troubles quickly when I saw several of the enemy some five miles on their side of the lines. Wanting to surprise them, I climbed up to the clouds and then through them. At first I went into what seemed a very sullen cloud, with dark grey and heavy mist all about me, the view being limited to a space of 10 feet. As I climbed higher up, the colour grew lighter and lighter until at last above me was nothing but blue sky and sunshine. The top of the clouds was as flat as a table. It looked as if one could land on it and sit there all day.

I kept flying along, carefully watching my compass to get the correct direction, also gazing at the beautiful cloud-pictures around me, when suddenly, just above, I heard the old wicked rattle of a pair of machine guns. Pulling up, I looked about and saw coming down straight on me from in front, three enemy scouts. The leader, to my great joy, I recognized as the man who had trapped me so badly in the fight just told of. He was well ahead of the other two, who were trailing behind him, and I knew, if I could only shoot well, I would have a chance to get him without being worried by the others, until they could reach the fight. On we came, head-on, both firing as fast as we could. I saw his smoking bullets going streaking by about 4 feet above my head, and what annoyed me a bit was the fact that they were passing that spot in a well-concen-

217

trated group, showing that he had his shooting well in hand and was quite cool. I have never fired with more care in my life. I took sight on the engine of his machine, knowing, if I hit it, some of the bullets would slide along its edge and get the pilot, who was just behind. On we came toward each other, at tremendous speed. I could see my bullets hitting his machine, and at the same instant his bullets scattered badly, so it was obvious he had become nervous and was not shooting as well as before. Suddenly he swerved, and tried to pass slightly to my left. I kept going straight at him, firing both guns. My bullets were all around the pilot's seat by this time and seemed to be hitting him. The next machine had come in now, firing at me, and too near for me to turn after the first one, so I turned toward the second Hun. My third opponent did not like the look of the fight, and kept well off to one side, diving away to escape a few seconds later. I looked over my shoulder to see what was happening to the first man, and was overjoyed to see his machine, a mass of flames and smoke, just commencing to fall. The second man I manœuvred with, doing almost two complete turns before being able to get in the shot I wanted. Then there was no trouble at all. With the first round he also burst into flames, and fell, following the other through the clouds. I looked for the third man, who had just dived away, anxious to wipe out the whole crowd. I dived after him. Down through the clouds we plunged, and, emerging, I saw he was well out of my reach, so I turned to watch my two victims. They were both falling within a thousand feet of each other, two flaming masses, crashing in death to the earth.

218

In a few days I was to go on another leave to England, so I put in every moment that I could in the air, trying to increase the number of machines to my credit. In this way, one evening, I came upon three, and managed to surprise them in the old way that I had done so often when I was flying a Nieuport. I dived on the rear and highest one, but found I did not have the patience to crawl up to my usual range. Two guns hardly made it necessary as before, so I opened fire at a little over 100 yards. As in the old days, there was no second stage to it at all—down he went completely out of control; and I stayed above, the other two having escaped, and watched him falling 8000 feet.

This was my forty-fifth victory, and the next day I had my forty-sixth and forty-seventh, in two fights shortly following one another.

It was the evening before I was to leave for England, and, to my great disgust, I had been unable to catch sight of a single German. So I flew north to watch a Canadian attack at Lens. There was a great battle going on, and for fifteen minutes I watched it raging. Then, chancing to look up above me, I saw a two-seater of the enemy coming toward our lines. It really seemed to be just a godsend, so I went straight at him almost head-on—that is, coming up slightly from below, but in front of him. I fired at him as I came, and as no result appeared, when I was 100 yards away, I dived and came up, pointing my nose straight up into the sky, as he flew across over me. Then I fired again. Suddenly the planes on one side of the Hun appeared to break and fall back, then to sweep away entirely, and the machine fell in fragments. It was not a nice sight. I had

219

evidently hit the machine in a lucky place, which had caused it to break, but in all probability the occupants were still alive. However, it was not for me to pity them at that stage of the game, and I could not put them out of their misery, so I remained above and watched them fall.

Two scouts had appeared just before I attacked this two-seater, but when I went toward them they had flown away. A minute later I saw them flying toward me. They did not want to fight, though, and turned away, heading in an easterly direction. The range was too far for me to open fire, so I chased them a bit, a distance of about two miles. They managed to keep 300 yards away, and as the wind was blowing me into Germany at the rate of sixty miles an hour, besides my own speed, I decided it was not worth while. Before leaving off the chase I thought I might as well send a few shots after them, as it might be my last chance to fight in France. I took very careful aim on the rear machine and opened fire. The Hun suddenly went into a spinning nose-dive and fell toward earth. I did not think for a moment I had hit him at that range, but watched to see just what game the German was playing. Down he went all the way from 13,000 feet to the ground, and crashed—a complete wreck. A lucky bullet must have hit the pilot and killed him instantly. It was indeed my last fight in France, and the next day I went to England on leave, and also to attend an investiture at Buckingham Palace, at which I was to receive all three of my decorations.

CHAPTER 22

WHEN I LEFT the aerodrome to start for England I had a vague feeling I would not be back again. I had heard nothing more about my transfer, but the very fact that there was a great deal of uncertainty made me anxious, and I remember, when leaving the old place, turning around to have a last look at it. I was lucky to find a car going all the way to Boulogne that day, and with four others, one of whom was going back to England for good, made the trip. On the way we stopped at a village where there was a famous farm for French police-dogs. We spent an interesting hour there, while the French lady who owned the dogs showed us all around her beautiful place. The dogs were of all ages, from two-week old puppies to full French champions. We left there just in time to reach Boulogne for luncheon—my last meal in France, as I managed to catch a boat for England at 2 o'clock.

Eight o'clock that night saw me in London, and I was certainly glad to get there. At 9 o'clock I was in the middle of a big dinner, given by several of my friends, after which we went to a dance. It seemed years since I had been near London, and every sight and every sound was joyful to me. A few days later, though, I left town and went to the country.

About this time word came through that I was not going back to France. I was very disappointed. I reported for duty, but was given a few weeks' more leave in which to rest. During this time I went to the investiture by the King. I had, on the previous day, received a telegram of instructions, telling me to report at Buckingham Palace at 10.30 in the morning dressed in service uniform. At 10.10 I was there, not wishing to be behind time on such an occasion, and realizing I had better find out before it happened just what was expected of me. Walking into the Palace I came to a hat-stand, where everybody was checking things. I handed in my hat, gloves, and stick, whereupon I was told to hang on to the gloves, wearing one on my left hand and carrying the other. Then, following a number of other officers, also there to be decorated, I came to a room in which a General was standing. I asked him where I was to go, and he asked me what I was getting. I began the long rigmarole of V.C., D.S.O., and M.C., but before I had finished he told me to go in with the D.S.O.s, as I was the only V.C. So I slipped away into a room where there were about 150 other officers. After waiting there for over half an hour, another General came in, and gave us explicit instructions as to what to do in the King's presence. It was a terrible moment for all of us.

Finally, the doors opened and we headed towards the room in which the King was standing with his staff. Following some Generals and Colonels, who were being admitted to the Order of St. Michael and St. George, it came to my turn to march in. I knew my instructions well. Ten yards across to the middle of the room, and then a turn to the left and bow. Imagine my consternation, when, at the first of those ten paces, one of my boots began to squeak. Somehow or other I managed to get to the proper

222

place, where I was facing His Majesty. Here I had to listen to an account of my own deeds, read by one of the staff, while I myself stood stiffly at attention. Then, approaching the King, he hooked three medals on my breast. These had been handed to him on a cushion. He congratulated me on winning them, and said it was the first time he had been able to give all three to any one person.

After a short, one-sided conversation, in which my only attempt to speak failed utterly, although all I was trying to say was "Yes, sir," he shook hands with me, and I bowed and backed away, turning and walking thirty squeaky paces to a door in the corner of the room. The moment I reached the outside of this door I thought I had been thrown into the arms of a highway robber. A man suddenly stepped from one side, and before I could stop him had snatched the three glittering medals off my chest, and was fifteen yards ahead of me on the way down the hall before I realized what had happened. I took after him, not knowing what to do, but he picked up three boxes from a table, put the medals in, and handed them back to me. Then he returned to meet the next man coming out, who incidentally was a great friend of mine and also in the Flying Corps. The next thing to be feared was the crowd at the Palace gates, and the photographers. Luckily, I had a car waiting in the enclosure, and thus managed to evade everybody.

A week later I was promoted to the rank of Major, and also learned that I had been awarded a bar to my Distinguished Service Order ribbon. Good news, like bad luck, never comes singly. A few days after that I heard I had been granted permission to go home to Canada for a visit. The notice was short, but within eighteen hours I had made all arrangements, and was on a train to catch the boat sailing from Liverpool next day. Within two weeks I was home.

APPENDIX

CHRONOLOGICAL SUMMARY OF THE WAR—
WESTERN FRONT AND OTHER SIGNIFICANT DATES

1914

June

28—Archduke Francis Ferdinand, heir to throne of Austria-Hungary, assassinated at Sarajevo, Bosnia.

July

18—Aviation Section of the U. S. Army's Signal Corps authorized by Congress.
28—Austria-Hungary declares war on Serbia.
29—Russia mobilizes.

August

1—Germany declares war on Russia. France mobilizes.
2—Germany invades Luxembourg.
3—Germany declares war on France.
4—Germany invades Belgium. Halted at Liège. Great Britain at war with Germany.
5—President Wilson tenders good offices of United States in interests of peace.
6—Austria-Hungary at war with Russia.

7—French invade Alsace. Marshal Joffre in supreme command of French army. Montenegro at war with Austria. British Expeditionary Force lands at Ostend, Calais, and Dunkirk.

8—Serbia at war with Germany. Portugal announces readiness to stand by alliance with England.

12—France and Great Britain at war with Austria-Hungary. Montenegro at war with Germany.

13-15—British RFC Squadrons fly to France.

17—Belgian capital removed from Brussels to Antwerp. Liège captured by Germans.

19—Canadian Parliament authorizes raising expeditionary force. First RFC air reconnaissance patrol over the Western Front.

20—Germans occupy Brussels.

21—Battle of Charleroi.

22—RFC air reconnaissance patrol reports Von Kluck's enemy force advancing on British front.

23—British at Battle of Mons.

24—Germans enter France near Lille.

25—Three RFC planes force down first German aircraft.

26—Louvain sacked and burned by Germans. Viviani Premier of France.

28—Austria declares war on Belgium.

29—Russians invest Königsberg, East Prussia.

30—Amiens occupied by Germans.

31—Russian army in East Prussia defeated at Tannenberg by Germans under Von Hindenburg.

September

3—Paris in state of siege; government transferred to Bordeaux.

4—Germans occupy Rheims.

6-10—Battle of Marne. Von Kluck beaten by Marshal Joffre. German army retreats from Paris to Soissons-Rheims line.

226

14—French re-occupy Amiens and Rheims.
20—Rheims cathedral shelled by Germans.
24—Allies occupy Peronne.
29—Antwerp bombardment begins.

October

2—British Admiralty announces intention to mine North Sea areas.
9—Antwerp surrenders to Germans. Government removed to Ostend.
13—British occupy Ypres.
14—Canadian Expeditionary Force of 32,000 men lands at Plymouth.
15—Germans occupy Ostend. Belgian government removed to Havre, France.

December

14—First Battle of Champagne.
16—German squadron bombards Hartlepool, Scarborough, and Whitby on cast coast of England.

1915

January

Allied flyer shoots down German plane with a rifle in the first aerial duel of the war.

February

French Lieutenant Roland Garros downs enemy aircraft with fixed machine gun firing between propeller blades.
10—Russians defeated by Germans in Battle of Masurian Lakes.

18—German submarines begin "blockade" of British Isles.
19–20—First German Zeppelin raid on England.

March

Anthony Fokker perfects synchronized machine gun.
10—British take Neuve Chapelle in Flanders.

April

22—Second Battle of Ypres. Poison gas first used by Germans
in attack on Canadians.

May

7—*Lusitania,* Cunard liner, sunk by German submarine off
Kinsale Head, Irish coast, with loss of 1152 lives; 102
Americans.
23—Italy declares war on Austria-Hungary and begins in-
vasion on a 60-mile front.
31—German Zeppelins bomb London for first time.

June

4–6—German aircraft bombs English towns.
7—RNAS Flight Sub-Lieutenant R. A. J. Warneford shoots
down Zeppelin over Belgium.
15—Allied aircraft bombs Karlsruhe, in retaliation for raids
on England.

July

31—Baden bombed by French aircraft.

August

12—First enemy ship torpedoed and sunk by British seaplane
at the Dardanelles.

19—Colonel "Boom" Trenchard placed in command of the RFC in France.

September

25—Allies open Artois offensive and occupy Lens.

October

12—Edith Cavell, English nurse, shot by Germans for aiding British prisoners to escape from Belgium.
13—London bombed by Zeppelins; 55 persons killed; 114 injured.
14—Bulgaria at war with Serbia.
15—Great Britain declares war on Bulgaria.
17—France at war with Bulgaria.
19—Italy and Russia at war with Bulgaria.
29—Briand becomes Premier of France, succeeding Viviani.

November

17—Anglo-French war council hold first meeting in Paris.

December

15—General Sir Douglas Haig succeeds Field Marshal Sir John French as Commander-in-Chief of British forces in France.

1916

January

29–31—German Zeppelins bomb Paris and towns in England.

February

10—British conscription law goes into effect.

21—Battle of Verdun begins. Germans take Haumont. Organize *Escadrille Americaine*, N. 124 (later known as Lafayette Escadrille).

25—Fort Douaumont falls to Germans.

March

9—Germany declares war on Portugal on the latter's refusal to give up seized ships.

15—Austria-Hungary at war with Portugal.

31—Melancourt taken by Germans in Battle of Verdun.

April

French arm Nieuport 11s with Le Prieur air-to-air rockets. Successfully down Zeppelin.

19—President Wilson publicly warns Germany not to pursue submarine policies.

20—Russian troops landed at Marseilles for service on French front. Sergeant Elliot Cowdin first American awarded French *Medaille Militaire*.

May

15—Vimy Ridge gained by British.

22—French fighter pilots down 5 German observation balloons with Le Prieur rockets.

31—Battle of Jutland; British and German fleets engaged; heavy losses on both sides.

June

5—Kitchener, British Secretary of War, loses life when cruiser *Hampshire* is sunk off the Orkney Islands.

6—Germans capture Fort Vaux in Verdun attack.

18—First American shot down, H. Clyde Balsley of the Lafayette Escadrille.

230

July

1—British and French attack north and south of the Somme.
14—British Cavalry penetrate German second line.
15—Longueval captured by British.
25—Pozieres occupied by British.
30—British and French advance between Delville Wood and the Somme.

August

3—French recapture Fleury.
27—Rumania declares war on Austria-Hungary.
28—Italy at war with Germany.
28—Germany at war with Rumania.
31—Bulgaria at war with Rumania. Turkey at war with Rumania.

September

2–3—Lieutenant W. Leefe Robinson first to shoot down Zeppelin over England.
15—British capture Flers, Courcelette, and other German positions on Western Front, using "tanks."
26—Combles and Thiepval captured by British and French.

October

24—Fort Douaumont recaptured by French.

November

2—Fort Vaux evacuated by Germans.
7—Woodrow Wilson re-elected President of the United States.
13—British advance along the Ancre.
22—Emperor Franz Josef of Austria-Hungary dies. Succeeded by Charles I.
23—German warships bombard English coast.
28—First German seaplane raid on London.

December

7—David Lloyd George succeeds Asquith as Prime Minister of England.

15—French complete recapture of ground taken by Germans in Battle of Verdun.

18—President Wilson makes peace overtures to belligerents.

26—Germany replies to President's note and suggests a peace conference.

30—French government on behalf of Allies replies to President Wilson's note and refuses to discuss peace till Germany agrees to give "restitution, reparation and guarantees."

1917

January

22—President Wilson suggests to the belligerents a "peace without victory."

31—Germany announces unrestricted submarine warfare.

February

3—United States severs diplomatic relations with Germany. Count Von Bernstorff is handed his passport.

17—British troops on the Ancre capture German positions.

28—United States makes public a communication from Germany to Mexico proposing an alliance, and offering as a reward the return of Mexico's lost territory in Texas, New Mexico, and Arizona (Zimmerman Telegram). Submarine campaign of Germans results in the sinking of 134 vessels during February.

March

3—British advance on Bapaume.

4—Germans begin withdrawal along Hindenburg Line.

14—China breaks with Germany.

15—Czar Nicholas abdicates. Prince Lvoff heads new cabinet.

17—Bapaume falls to British. Roye and Lassigny occupied by French.

18—Peronne, Chaulnes, Nesle, and Noyon evacuated by Germans, who retreat on an 85-mile front.

19—Alexander Ribot becomes French Premier, succeeding Briand.

26–31—British advance on Cambrai.

April

6—United States declares war on Germany.

7—Cuba and Panama at war with Germany.

8—Austria-Hungary breaks with United States.

9—Germans retreat before British on long front (Battle of Arras).

9—Bolivia breaks with Germany.

13—Vimy, Givenchy, Bailleul, and positions about Lens taken by Canadians.

20—Turkey breaks with United States.

30—Major William C. Mitchell, first American officer to cross enemy lines.

May

7—German bombers make first night raid on London.

9—Liberia breaks with Germany.

15—Marshal Pétain succeeds Marshal Nivelle as Commander-in-Chief of French armies.

16—Bullecourt captured by British in the Battle of Arras.

17—Honduras breaks with Germany.

18—Conscription bill signed by President Wilson.

19—Nicaragua breaks with Germany.

20—British seaplane sinks first submarine from the air.

25—Twenty-one Gotha bombers make first mass daylight attack on England. 200 casualties.

June

2—Aviation Section redesignated Airplane Division, Signal Corps.

5—Registration day for new draft army in United States.

7—Messines-Wytschaete ridge in English hands.

8—General Pershing, Commander-in-Chief of American Expeditionary Force (AEF), arrives in England en route to France.

13—588 casualties in first mass daylight raid on London by 14 Gothas.

18—Haiti breaks with Germany.

30—Lieutenant Colonel Billy Mitchell replaces Major Dodd as Aviation Officer, American Expeditionary Force.

July

1—Russians begin offensive in Gallicia. Kerensky, minister of war, leading in person.

3—AEF arrives in France.

4—First 8-cylinder Liberty engine, designed and built in 6 weeks, ready for testing.

6—Canadian House of Commons passes Compulsory Military Service Bill.

12—King Constantine of Greece abdicates in favour of his second son, Alexander.

16–23—Retreat of Russians on a front of 155 miles.

20—Drawing of draft numbers for American conscript army begins. Alexander Kerensky becomes Russian Premier, succeeding Lvoff.

22—Siam at war with Germany and Austria.

23—Major Benjamin D. Foulois appointed officer-in-charge Aeroplane Division.

24—$640 million appropriated to expand Aeroplane Division to 9989 officers and 87,083 men.

27—British DH-4 arrives in United States to serve as production model.

August

2—Sopwith Pup successfully landed on deck of H.M.S. *Furious*.
7—Liberia at war with Germany.
8—Canadian Conscription Bill passes its third reading in Senate.
13—First Aero Squadron leaves England to join AEF in France.
14—China at war with Germany and Austria-Hungary.
15—St. Quentin Cathedral destroyed by Germans.
15—Canadian troops capture Hill 70, dominating Lens.

September

5—New American National Army begins to assemble.
14—Painleve becomes French Premier, succeeding Ribot.
16—Russia proclaimed a republic by Kerensky.
20—Costa Rica breaks with Germany.
25—Guynemer killed.
26—Zonnebeke, Polygon Wood, and Tower Hamlets, east of Ypres, taken by British.

October

6—Peru and Uruguay break with Germany.
9—Poelcapelle and other German positions captured in Franco-British attack.
18—DH-4s ordered into mass production (4500 were built by the end of the war of which 1213 reached the front).
23—American troops in France fire their first shot in trench warfare. French advance northeast of Soissons.
26—Brazil at war with Germany.
29—First American-built DH-4 flight-tested at Dayton, Ohio.

November

1—Germans abandon position on Chemin des Dames.

3—Americans in trenches suffer 20 casualties in German attacks.

6—Passchendaele captured by Canadians.

7—The Russian Bolsheviks, led by Lenin and Trotsky, seize Petrograd and depose Kerensky.

9—Italians retreat to the Piave.

10—Lenin becomes Premier of Russia, succeeding Kerensky.

15—Georges Clemenceau becomes Premier of France, succeeding Painleve.

21—Ribecourt, Flesquieres, Havrincourt, Marcoing, and other German positions captured by the British.

23—Italians repulse Germans on the whole front from the Asiago Plateau to the Brenta River.

24—Battle of Cambrai. British tanks approach within three miles, capturing Bourlon Wood.

27—Brigadier General B. D. Foulois replaces Brigadier General William L. Kenly as Chief of Air Service, AEF.

December

1—German East Africa reported completely conquered. Allies' Supreme War Council, representing the United States, France, Great Britain, and Italy, holds first meeting at Versailles.

3—Russian Bolsheviks arrange armistice with Germans.

5—British retire from Bourlon Wood, Graincourt, and other positions west of Cambrai.

7—Finland declares independence.

8—Jerusalem, held by the Turks for 673 years, surrenders to British, under General Allenby.

8—Ecuador breaks with Germany.

10—Panama at war with Austria-Hungary.

11—United States at war with Austria-Hungary.

236

15—Armistice signed between Germany and Russia at Brest-
Litovsk.
17—Coalition government of Sir Robert Borden is returned and
conscription confirmed in Canada.
26—The Curtiss JN-4 "Jenny" becomes basic trainer for
American pilots.

1918

January

2—British Air Ministry formed.
8—President Wilson proclaimed his "Fourteen Points."
18—Major General Sir John Salmond succeeds Major General
Sir Hugh "Boom" Trenchard as commander of the RFC,
BEF.
19—American troops take over sector northwest of Toul.
20—Colonel Billy Mitchell, Chief of Air Service, I Army Corps.
23—First AEF observation balloon ascends in France.

February

1—Argentine Minister of War recalls military attachés from
Berlin and Vienna.
18—103rd Aero Squadron, AEF, made up of former members
of the Lafayette Escadrille, begins operations at the front.
22—American troops in Chemin des Dames sector.
26—First U. S. Air Service unit to serve with American troops
at the front was the 2nd Balloon Co.

March

1—Americans gain signal victory in salient north of Toul.
3—Peace treaty between Bolshevik government of Russia and
the Central Powers signed at Brest-Litovsk.

237

4—Treaty signed between Germany and Finland.

5—Rumania signs preliminary treaty of peace with Central Powers.

9—Russian capital moved from Petrograd to Moscow.

11—Lieutenant Paul Baer of 103rd Aero Squadron awarded first Air Service Distinguished Service Cross.

14—Russo-German peace treaty ratified by All-Russian Congress of Soviets at Moscow. Patrol by the 95th Aero Squadron constitutes first air action of the 1st Pursuit Group.

19—Pilots of the 94th (Hat-in-the-Ring) Squadron fly first operational flights across the lines.

21—Germans begin great drive on 50-mile front from Arras to La Fere. Bombardment of Paris by German long-range gun from a distance of 76 miles.

24—Peronne, Ham, and Chauny evacuated by Allies.

25—Bapaume and Nesle occupied by Germans.

29—Marshal Foch chosen Commander-in-Chief of all Allied armies on the Western Front.

April

1—The RFC and RNAS combined to form the Royal Air Force (RAF).

9—Second German drive begun in Flanders.

10—First German drive halted before Amiens, after maximum advance of 35 miles.

14—Lieutenant Douglas Campbell, 94th Aero Squadron, scores the first victory as an American trained pilot.

15—Second German drive halted before Ypres, after maximum advance of 10 miles.

21—Guatemala at war with Germany.

22—Baron von Richthofen, top ranking German flyer, killed.

23—British naval forces raid German submarine base in Zeebrugge, Belgium, and block channel. First United States shipment of Liberty engines arrives in France.

238

29—Lieutenant Edward V. Rickenbacker shoots down first German plane.

May

7—Nicaragua at war with Germany and her allies.
11—First American-built DH-4 powered by a Liberty engine delivered to the AEF. First flight in France made on May 17.
19—Major Raoul Lufbery, famous American aviator, killed.
20—Army Aviation separated from the Signal Corps.
24—Costa Rica at war with Germany and Austria-Hungary. 6 HS-1s, American Navy-built seaplanes first to arrive in France.
27—Third German drive begins on Aisne-Marne front of 30 miles between Soissons and Rheims.
28—Germans sweep on beyond the Chemin des Dames and cross the Vesle at Fismes. Cantigny taken by Americans in local attack.
29—Soissons evacuated by French. Brigadier General Mason M. Patrick becomes new Chief of Air Service, AEF.
31—Marne River crossed by Germans, who reach Chateau Thierry, 40 miles from Paris.

June

3–6—American Marines and soldiers check advance of Germans at Chateau Thierry and Neuilly after maximum advance of Germans 32 miles. Beginning of American co-operation on major scale.
5—Major General Sir Hugh Trenchard commands British Independent Air Force for strategic bombing of Germany.
9–14—German drive on Western Front ended.
12—First day United States day bombing by 96th Aero Squadron on railroad marshalling yards in France.
15–24—Austrian drive on Italian front ends in complete failure.
30—American troops in France number 1,019,115.

July

1—Vaux taken by Americans.

3—Mohammed V, Sultan of Turkey, dies.

10—Czecho-Slovaks, aided by Allies, take control of a long stretch of the Trans-Siberian Railway.

15—Haiti at war with Germany. Defence of Chateau Thierry blocks new German drive on Paris.

17—Lieutenant Quentin Roosevelt, youngest son of ex-President Theodore Roosevelt, killed in aerial battle near Chateau Thierry.

18—French and Americans begin counter-offensive on Marne-Aisne front.

20—U. S. 148th Aero Squadron begins operation with the RAF near Dunkirk.

23—French take Oulchy-le-Chateau and drive the Germans back ten miles between the Aisne and the Marne.

30—Allies astride the Ourcq; Germans in full retreat to the Vesle.

August

1—Sergeant Joyce Kilmer, American poet and critic, aged 31, dies in battle.

2—French troops recapture Soissons. 18 United States-built DH-4s with Liberty engines fly their first patrol along the front.

3—President Wilson announces new policy regarding Russia and agrees to co-operate with Great Britain, France, and Japan in sending forces to Murmansk, Archangel, and Vladivostok.

3—Allies sweep on between Soissons and Rheims, driving the enemy from his base at Fismes and capturing the entire Aisne-Vesle front.

7—Franco-American troops cross the Vesle.

8—New Allied drive begun by British Field Marshal Haig in Picardy, penetrating enemy front 14 miles.

10—Montdidier recaptured.

13—Lassigny *massif* taken by French.

15—Canadians capture Damery and Parvillers, northwest of Roye.

29—Noyon and Bapaume fall in new Allied advance.

September

1—Australians take Peronne. Americans fight for the first time on Belgian soil and capture Voormezeele.

11—Germans are driven back to the Hindenburg Line which they held in November 1917.

12—Registration day for new U.S. draft of men between 18 and 45. Lieutenant Frank Luke, the American "Balloon Buster," scored his first victory.

13—Americans begin vigorous offensive in St. Mihiel Sector on 40-mile front. 1481 Allied planes under command of Brigadier General Billy Mitchell, largest air armada ever assembled, participated in the offensive.

14—St. Mihiel recaptured from Germans. General Pershing announces entire St. Mihiel salient erased, liberating more than 150 square miles of French territory which had been in German hands since 1914.

25—British take 40,000 prisoners in Palestine offensive.

27—Franco-Americans in drive from Rheims to Verdun take 30,000 prisoners.

28—Belgians attack enemy from Ypres to North Sea, gaining four miles.

29—Bulgaria surrenders to General d'Esperey, the Allied commander.

30—British-Belgian advance reaches Roulers.

October

1—St. Quentin, cornerstone of Hindenburg Line, captured. Allies bomb Germans using electrical bomb release for first time. Damascus occupied by British in Palestine campaign.

2—Lens evacuated by Germans. The United States "Bug," guided missile, successfully flight-tested at Dayton.

3—Albania cleared of Austrians by Italians.

4—King Ferdinand of Bulgaria abdicates; Boris succeeds.

5—Prince Maximilian, new German Chancellor, pleads with President Wilson to ask Allies for armistice.

7—Berry-au-Bac taken by French.

9—Cambrai in Allied hands.

11—Americans advance through Argonne forest.

12—German foreign secretary, Solf, says plea for armistice is made in name of German people; agrees to evacuate all foreign soil. American pursuit pilots participate in first U.S. air night action.

13—Laon and La Fere abandoned by Germans. Grandpre captured by Americans after four days' battle.

14—President Wilson refers Germans to Marshal Foch for armistice terms. A British Handley-Page drops a 1650-pound bomb, largest of the war.

16—Lille entered by British patrols.

17—Ostend, German submarine base, taken by land and sea forces. Douai falls to Allies.

19—Bruges and Zeebrugge taken by Belgian and British forces.

25—Beginning of terrific Italian drive which nets 50,000 prisoners in five days.

26—"Boom" Trenchard appointed Commander-in-Chief, Inter-Allied Independent Air Force.

31—Turkey surrenders; armistice takes effect at noon; conditions include free passage of Dardanelles.

November

1—Clery-le-Grand captured by American First Army troops.

3—Americans sweep ahead on 50-mile front above Verdun; enemy in full retreat. German Fleet mutinies at Kiel. Official reports announce capture of 362,350 Germans since July 15. Austria surrenders, signing armistice with Italy at 3 P.M. after 500,000 prisoners had been taken.

4—Americans advance beyond Stenay and strike at Sedan.

7—American Rainbow Division and parts of First Division enter suburbs of Sedan.

8—Heights south of Sedan seized by Americans.

9—Maubeuge captured by Allies.

10—Canadians take Mons in irresistible advance. The 3rd Pursuit Group flies last American patrol over enemy lines.

11—Germany surrenders; armistice takes effect at 11 A.M. American flag hoisted on Sedan front.

RECORD OF SERVICE

Lieut. Colonel W. A. Bishop, VC, MC, DSO, DFC, etc.

Fig. 1. Royal Flying Corps badge (top); RFC uniform button (bottom)

Fig. 2. RFC observer's wing insignia worn by Bishop

Fig. 3. Royal Canadian Air Force badge (top); Royal
Air Force badge (bottom)

Appointments

	DAY	MONTH	YEAR
Lieut. 9th Mississauga Horse	30	9	14
Left Canada, 7th C.M.R., Lieutenant	9	6	15
Trans. to Base Details, 2nd Div. Cav.	3	9	15

	DAY	MONTH	YEAR

T.O.S. General List, France on arrival in
France & remains attd. to RFC 18–1–16

S.O.S. General List, France on being
admitted to Hosp. in England 11–5–16

TO BE FLYING OFFICER
(OBSERVER) 15–11–16

Seniority from 18–1–16

SECONDED FOR DUTY WITH RFC 15–11–16

TO BE FLYING OFFICER RFC MIL.
WING. 8–12–16

Arrived in France for duty with RFC &
attached 60th Sqdn. 7–3–17

TO BE FLIGHT COMMANDER & TO BE
TEMP. CAPT. WHILE SO EMPLOYED 8–4–17

TO BE TEMP. CAPTAIN, CANADIAN
GENERAL LIST 8–4–17

TO BE CHIEF INSTRUCTOR, SCHOOL OF
AERIAL GUNNERY & TO BE TEMP.
MAJOR WHILST SO EMPLOYED
GRADED AS SQDN. COMMANDER
from FLIGHT COMDR. 28–8–17

Trans. to Home Estab. RFC & posted to
C.C.R.D. 1–9–17

TO BE SQDN. COMDR. FROM A CHIEF
INSTR. (GRADED AS A SQDN. COMDR.)
SCHOOLS OF AERIAL GUNNERY, AND
TO RETAIN HIS TEMP. RANK WHILST
SO EMPLOYED. 13–3–18

with seniority from 28–8–17

246

	DAY	MONTH	YEAR

CEASES TO BE SECONDED FOR DUTY
WITH RAF   5–8–18
TO BE TEMP. LIEUT-COLONEL,
CANADIAN CAVALRY   5–8–18
APPOINTED G.S.O. 1st Grade, General Staff   5–8–18
RELINQUISHES HIS COMMISSION IN
RAF ON CEASING TO BE
EMPLOYED   5–8–18
Attached to H.Q., O.M.F. of C. (Gen. Staff)   5–8–18
Proceeded on duty to Canada   3–10–18
Returned from Canada   17–11–18
RELINQUISHES APPT. G.S.O. 1st Grade   2–12–18
T.O.S., NO. 2 D.D., Toronto   3–12–18
S.O.S., O.M.F. of C., on transfer to C.E.F.
in Canada, upon cessation of hostilities   7–12–18
S.O.S., C.E.F. in Canada, on General
Demobilization   31–12–18

Some of the entries may be somewhat puzzling. To the best of our knowledge Bishop was attached to the RFC on 1 September 1915 and seems to have finished his observer training in November or December of 1915. You will note, however, that he was not officially gazetted a Flying Officer (Observer) until a year later, although the appointment had seniority as of January 18, 1916.

Blue

White

Red

White

SQUADRON POSTINGS AND ASSIGNMENTS

No. 21 Sqn	2 Sept 1915
No. 37 (HD) Sqn	8 Dec 1916
No. 60 Sqn	7 Mar 1917
No. 85 Sqn	22 May 1918

HONOURS AND AWARDS

M.C.	(auth. London Gazette ✻ 30095, dated 26-5-17)
D.S.O.	(" " " " 30135 " 18-6-17)
V.C.	(" " " " 30228 " 11-8-17)
Bar to D.S.O.	(" " " " 30308 " 25-9-17)

MENTIONED in Sir D. Haig's Despatch of 7-11-17
(auth. London Gazette ✻ 30421, dated 11-12-17)

D.F.C.	(" " " " 30827 " 3-8-18)
	(" " " " 30775 " 2-7-18)

Croix de Guerre "with Palme"
(auth. London Gazette ✻ 30989, dated 2-11-18)
Croix de Chevalier, Legion of Honor
(auth. London Gazette ✻ 30989, dated 2-11-18)

248

1917

Number	Date	Type Enemy Aircraft Destroyed
1	25 March	Albatross
2	31 March	Albatross (red)
3	7 April	Albatross
4	8 April	Albatross
5	8 April	Unidentified 2-Seater
6	8 April	Unidentified 1-Seater
7	20 April	Aviatik 2-Seater
8	22 April	Albatross
9	22 April	Albatross
10	23 April	Unidentified 2-Seater
11	23 April	Albatross
12	29 April	Albatross
13	30 April	Unidentified 2-Seater
14	30 April	Unidentified 2-Seater
15	2 May	Unidentified 2-Seater
16	2 May	Unidentified 2-Seater
17	4 May	Unidentified 2-Seater
18	7 May	Albatross (green and red)
19	7 May	Albatross (red)
20	26 May	Albatross
21	27 May	Aviatik 2-Seater (red and yellow)
22	31 May	Albatross
23	2 June	Albatross
24	2 June	Albatross
25	2 June	Albatross

249

Number	Date	Type Enemy Aircraft Destroyed
26	8 June	Albatross (red)
27	24 June	Albatross
28	25 June	Albatross
29	26 June	Albatross
30	26 June	Albatross
31	28 June	Albatross
32	10 July	Albatross (bright green)
33	12 July	Albatross (green and yellow)
34	17 July	Albatross
35	17 July	Albatross
36	20 July	Albatross
37	28 July	Albatross
38	28 July	Albatross
39	5 August	Albatross
40	5 August	Albatross
41	6 August	Albatross
42	9 August	Unidentified 2-Seater
43	13 August	Albatross (silver)
44	13 August	Albatross
45	15 August	Albatross
46	16 August	Aviatik 2-Seater
47	16 August	Albatross

1918

48	27 May	Unidentified 2-Seater
49	28 May	Albatross
50	28 May	Albatross

Number	Date	Type Enemy Aircraft Destroyed
51	30 May	Unidentified 2-Seater
52	30 May	Albatross
53	30 May	Albatross
54	31 May	Pfalz
55	31 May	Pfalz
56	1 June	Pfalz (black)
57	2 June	Pfalz (black, white tail)
58	4 June	Albatross
59	4 June	Albatross
60	15 June	Pfalz
61	16 June	Pfalz
62	16 June	Pfalz
63	17 June	Unidentified 2-Seater
64	17 June	Albatross
65	17 June	Unidentified 2-Seater
66	18 June	Albatross (natural wood fuselage)
67	18 June	Albatross (natural wood fuselage)
68	19 June	Pfalz
69	19 June	Pfalz
70	19 June	Pfalz
71	19 June	Pfalz
72	19 June	Unidentified 2-Seater

THE TOP BRITISH ACES, 1914–18

Although the British did not officially recognize the "ace" designation, unofficially they considered ten victories as the minimum qualification rather than the five accepted by the other Allied powers and the Germans. There were, however, more than 550 British flyers who downed at least five enemy aircraft. These included representatives from the then British Empire (Canadians, Australians, Irish, New Zealanders, South Africans, etc.). Among these heroes there were also 19 Americans, some of whose names appear in *italics* below.

The following are only the very top of the British list who had twenty or more victories to their credits:

	Victories	*Squa*
Major Edward "Mick" Mannock	73	40, 74, 85
Lieutenant Colonel William A. Bishop	72	21, 37, 60, 85
Major Raymond R. Collishaw	60	10(N),* 13(N)
Major James T. B. McCudden	57	3, 20, 29, 66, 56
Captain A. W. Beauchamp-Proctor	54	84
Captain Donald R. MacLaren	54	46
Major William G. Barker	53	9, 4, 15, 28, 6
		139, 201
Major Phillip F. Fullard	53	24, 1
Captain Robert A. Little	47	8(N),* 203
Captain G. E. H. McElroy	46	24, 40
Captain Albert Ball	43	13, 11, 8, 60, 2
Major T. F. Hazell	41	1, 24, 203
Captain Ira "Taffy" Jones	40	10, 74

* Naval Squadron

	Victories	*Squadrons*
Major Roderic S. Dallas	39	1(N),* 40
Captain John Gilmore	37	1, 24, 203
Captain W. G. Claxton	37	41
Captain Henry W. Wollett	35	24, 43
Captain Frank G. Quigley	34	70
Captain Frank R. McCall	34	13, 41, 1
Major G. H. Bowman	32	29, 56, 41
Major Albert D. Carter	31	19
Captain J. L. M. White	31	65
Captain W. L. Jordan	31	22, 203
Captain B. M. Frew	30	45
Captain Cedric E. Howell	30	45
Major Andrew E. McKeever	30	11, 22
Captain S. M. Kinkead	30	201
Captain A. H. Cobby	29	4(AFC)†
Captain Henry G. Launchford	29	20
Captain Brunwin-Hales	27	56
Captain G. D. Gurden	27	22
Captain R. T. C. Hoidge	27	56, 1
Major G. C. Maxwell	27	56
Captain W. C. Campbell	26	1
Captain James A. Slater	26	64
Captain W. E. Staton	26	62
Major K. L. Caldwell	25	8, 60, 74
Major R. J. O. Compston	25	8(N),* 40
Captain John Leacraft	25	19
Captain R. A. Mayberry	25	56
Captain John Andrews	24	24, 66, 209
Captain W. E. Shields	24	41
Captain J. S. T. Fall	23	3(N),* 4(N), 9(N)
Captain A. Hepburn	23	24, 88
Captain D. Lattimer	23	20
Captain Francis McCubbin	23	46
Captain E. J. K. McLoughry	23	23, 4(AFC)†
Lieutenant A. P. F. Rhys Davids	23	56

* Naval Squadron
† Australian Flying Corps

	Victories	*Squadro*
Captain S. W. Rosevear	23	201
Captain H. A. Whistler	23	3, 80
Major C. D. Booker	22	8(N), 201
Captain Henry Burden	22	56
Major W. J. C. K. Cochrane-Patrick	22	70, 23, 60
Captain A. J. Cooper	22	24
Captain R. King	22	4
Captain W. C. Lambert	22	24
Captain E. R. Tempest	22	64
Lieutenant McK. Thompson	22	20
Captain C. J. Venter	21	29
Captain A. H. Cobby	21	4(AFC)†
Captain P. J. Clayson	21	1
Captain R. P. Minifie	21	1(N)*
Captain G. E. Thompson	21	46
Captain D. J. Bell	20	27, 3
Captain F. C. Falkenburg	20	84
Captain F. W. Gillette	20	—
Captain T. S. Harrison	20	29
Captain W. L. Harrison	20	40, 1
Captain E. C. Johnston	20	24, 88
Captain C. F. King	20	43
Flight Sub-Lieutenant John J. Malone	20	3(N)*
Captain I. D. R. McDonald	20	24
Lieutenant C. M. MacEwen	20	28
Major Gilbert W. Murlis-Green	20	17, 44, 151, 70
Major K. R. Park	20	48
Captain D. A. Stewart	20	70, 18
Major A. M. Wilkinson	20	48

* Naval Squadron
† Australian Flying Corps

254

LEADING ALLIED ACES

French

There were a total of 160 aces in the French Aviation Service. Following is a list of the leading five:

	Victories
Captain René Fonck	75
Captain Georges Guynemer	53
Lieutenant Charles Nungesser	45
Lieutenant Georges Madon	41
Lieutenant Maurice Boyeau	35

American

A total of 117 Americans shot down five or more enemy aircraft to become aces. This includes victories gained while serving with the French and British, but only those who eventually served in the U. S. Air Service are listed. Here are the first five:

	Victories
Captain Edward V. Rickenbacker	26
Lieutenant Frank Luke, Jr.	21
Major Raoul Lufbery	17
Major George A. Vaughn	13
Captain Field E. Kindley	12

Belgian

Tiny Belgium produced five aces.

	Victories
Major Willy Coppens	34
Lieutenant Edmond Thieffry	10
Adjutant André de Meulemeester	10
Captain F. Jacquet	7
Lieutenant Jan Olieslagers	6

Italian

Among the forty-three Italian flyers who qualified as aces were:

	Victories
Major Francesco Baracca	36
Lieutenant Silvio Scaroni	26
Major Pier Ruggiero Piccio	24
Lieutenant Flavio Barracchini	21
Captain Fulco Ruffo di Calabria	20

Russian

Because of the Russian Revolution and the loss and destruction of official records, the total number of Russian aces

will never be known. The following five head the list of
those whose records remained or were reconstructed.

	Victories
Captain Alexander Kazakov	17
Captain P. d'Argueeff	15
Lieutenant Commander Alexander de Seversky	13
Lieutenant I. Smirnoff	12
Lieutenant M. Safonov	11

LEADING ENEMY ACES

German

Heading the list of more than three hundred German aces was Rittmeister Manfred von Richthofen, also known as the "Red Baron" because of his all-red Fokker fighter. He was leader of the famous "Flying Circus" and was the top ranking ace of both sides—friend and foe—in the First World War.

	Victories
Captain Manfred von Richthofen	80
Lieutenant Ernst Udet	62
Lieutenant Erich Lowenhardt	56
Lieutenant Werner Voss	48
Captain Bruno Loerzer	45

Austro-Hungarian

Like the British, the Austro-Hungarians considered only those with ten or more victories as aces. However, some thirty of their pilots downed more than five enemy aircraft apiece.

	Victories
Captain Godwin Brumowski	40
Lieutenant Julius Arigi	32
Lieutenant Frank Linke-Crawford	30
Lieutenant Benno Fiala	29
Lieutenant Josef Kiss	19

AEROPLANES FLOWN BY BISHOP IN WORLD WAR I

Following is a listing of aircraft types which Bishop flew during the First World War. Not all were flown operationally and the list is probably incomplete:

Maurice Farman Shorthorn
Maurice Farman Longhorn
BE-2c
BE-2d
BE-2e
BE-12
BE-12a
Avro (type or types not specified)
Nieuport 17
Sopwith Pup
Sopwith Camel
Martinsyde (type or types not specified)
Sopwith Dolphin
SE-5 and 5a
Bristol Scout
Bristol Fighter
Fokkers (probably captured or trophy D-VIIs)

AIRCRAFT SPECIFICATIONS AND DATA

Nieuport 17

Single-seater scout (1916–17). Bishop scored thirty-six of his confirmed victories in this tiny French fighter plane. He flew it until July 28, 1917.

Engine — 110 hp Le Rhône rotary
Wingspan — 27 ft.   *Length* — 19 ft. 6 ins.
Weight — 1233 lbs. loaded
Speed — 107 mph
Ceiling — 17,400 ft.
Endurance — 2 hrs.
Armament — 1 Lewis gun mounted on upper wing, fired over propeller and could be raised or lowered but not swung from side to side or fixed synchronized Vickers

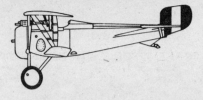

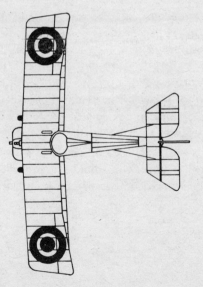

Fig. 5. Nieuport 17, three-view diagram

SE-5A

Single-seater scout (1917–18). This was an improvement over the SE-5, both of which were flown by Bishop. Three of the top British aces—Bishop, Mannock, and McCudden —scored most of their victories in these aircraft.

Engine — 200, 220, or 240 hp Hispano-Suiza; or 200 hp Wolseley Viper
Wingspan — 26 ft. 7½ ins.
                              Length — 20 ft. 11 ins.
Weight — 2048 lbs. loaded
Speed — 132 mph
Ceiling — 20,000 ft.
Endurance — 2 hrs. 30 min.
Armament — 1 fixed Vickers gun, and 1 Lewis machine gun mounted on upper wing, fired over propeller and could be raised or lowered but not swung from side to side

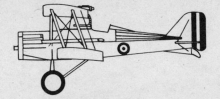

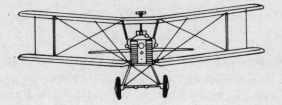

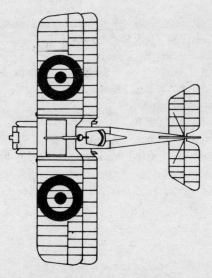

Fig. 6. SE-5A, three-view diagram

Sopwith Triplane

Single-seater scout (1917–18). This British fighter was flown by the Royal Naval Air Service, who swapped their Spad VIIs to the Royal Flying Corps for them. Canadian Ace Ray Collishaw led a flight of them—the famous "Black Flight."

Engine — 130 hp Clerget rotary
Wingspan — 26 ft. 7 ins.
                    Length — 18 ft. 10 ins.
Weight — 1415 lbs. loaded
Speed — 116 mph
Ceiling — 20,500 ft.
Endurance — 2 hrs. 15 min.
Armament — 1 fixed Vickers machine gun

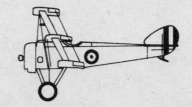

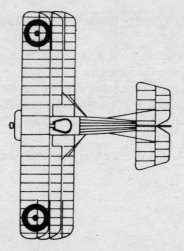

Fig. 7. Sopwith Triplane, three-view diagram

Sopwith Camel

Single-seater scout (1917–18). More enemy aircraft were destroyed by this British fighter than by any other in the First World War. It was flown by Canadian Captain Roy Brown in the action in which Von Richthofen was shot down.

Engine — 110 hp Le Rhône rotary or 130 hp Clerget rotary

Wingspan — 28 ft.   *Length* — 18 ft. 8 ins.

Weight — 1453 lbs. loaded

Speed — 119 mph (Le Rhône), 113 mph (Clerget)

Ceiling — 24,000 ft. (Le Rhône), 19,000 ft. (Clerget)

Endurance — 2 hrs. 45 min. (Le Rhône), 2 hrs. 30 min. (Clerget)

Armament — 2 fixed Vickers machine guns

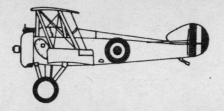

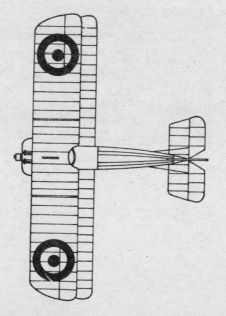

Fig. 8. Sopwith Camel, three-view diagram

Pfalz D-III

Single-seater scout (1917). The Pfalz together with the Albatross made up the bulk of Bishop's victories. These two German fighter types were very similar in appearance and, in fact, were grouped together within the same squadrons.

Engine — 160 hp Mercedes
Wingspan — 30 ft. 11 ins.

Length — 23 ft. 2 ins.

Weight — 2056 lbs. loaded
Speed — 103 mph
Ceiling — 17,580 ft.
Endurance — 2 hrs. 30 min.
Armament — 2 fixed Spandau machine guns

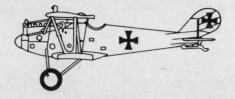

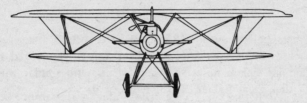

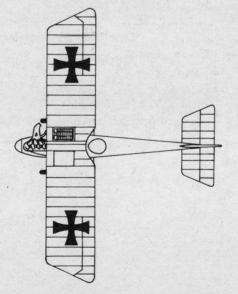

Fig. 9. Pfalz D-III, three-view diagram

Pfalz D-XII

Single-seater scout (1918). It appeared at the Front several months before the famous Fokker D-VII yet it had the familiar square nose, "N"-shape struts, and similar wings of that great fighter, which replaced it.

Engine — 180 or 200 hp Mercedes
Wingspan — 29 ft. 6 ins.
                              Length — 21 ft. 5 ins.
Weight — 1930 lbs. loaded
Speed — 125 mph (200 hp)
Ceiling — 18,000 ft.
Endurance — 1 hr. 30 min. to 2 hrs.
Armament — 2 fixed Spandau machine guns

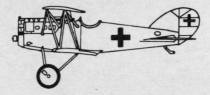

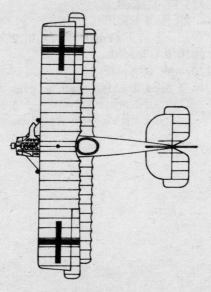

Fig. 10. Pfalz D-XII, three-view diagram

Albatross D-V

Single-seater scout of early 1917, one of the most successful of its line. It replaced the earlier excellent D-I of 1916. The D-III was itself replaced by the D-V, which resembled it closely in physical appearance, later in 1917.

Engine — 175 hp Mercedes
Wingspan — 29 ft. 7 ins.

                                  Length — 24 ft. 2 ins.

Weight — 2050 lbs. loaded
Speed — 120 mph at sea level
Armament — 2 fixed Spandau machine guns

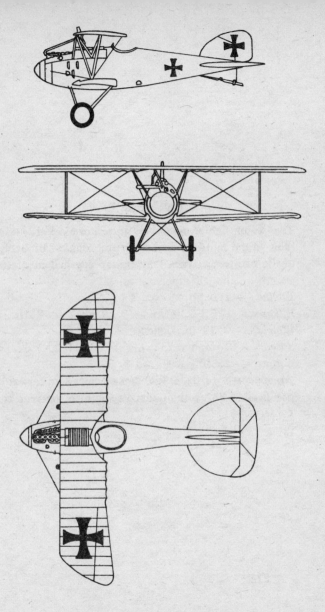

Fig. 11. Albatross D-V, three-view diagram

Halberstadt CL-II

Two-seater fighter reconnaissance plane (1917) comparable to the fabulous British Bristol Fighter. Probably one of the two-seater types that Bishop engaged in combat.

Engine — 180 hp Mercedes
Wingspan — 35 ft. 4 ins.   *Length* — 24 ft.
Weight — 2532 lbs. loaded
Speed — 97 mph
Ceiling — 13,500 ft.
Armament — 1 fixed Spandau machine gun forward, and one flexible Parabellum machine gun in the rear cockpit (observer's)

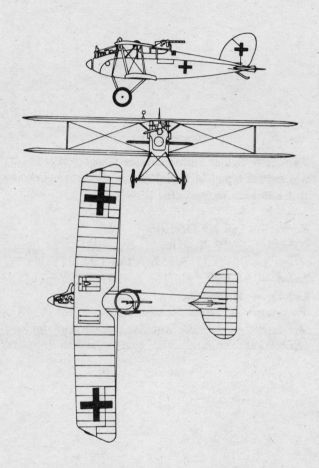

Fig. 12. Halberstadt CL-II, three-view diagram

Hannoveraner CL-III

Two-seater fighter reconnaissance plane (1917–18). This was another type which Bishop possibly met and downed. It had a unique biplane tail.

Engine — 180 hp Opel-Argus
Wingspan — 39 ft. 2 ins.
       Length — 25 ft. 6 ins.
Speed — 96 mph
Ceiling — 16,500 ft.
Endurance — 2 hrs. 30 min.
Armament — 1 fixed Spandau machine gun forward, 1 flexible Parabellum machine gun in the rear (observer's)

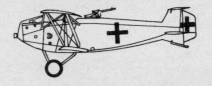

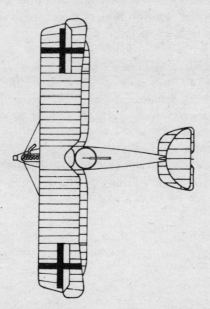

Fig. 13. Hannoveraner CL-III, three-view diagram

Aviatik C-II

Two-seater reconnaissance bomber (1915–16), a C-V model introduced in 1917 resembled the earlier model and showed little improvement. Both of these models may have been among Bishop's victims.

Engine — 160 hp Mercedes
Wingspan — 40 ft. 8 ins.   *Length* — 26 ft.
Weight — 2831 lbs. loaded
Speed — 82 mph at sea level, 66 mph at 9000 ft.
Ceiling — 11,500 ft.
Endurance — 4 hrs. 30 min.
Armament — 1 fixed synchronized Spandau machine gun, 1 flexible Parabellum machine gun in rear

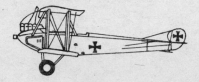

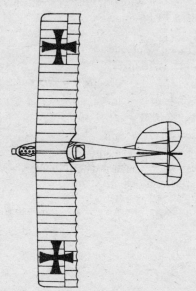

Fig. 14. Aviatik C-II, three-view diagram

Rumpler C-V

Two-seater reconnaissance (1917–18) developed from the C-III model of 1916. Although he did not engage many two-seaters, those too may have traded shots with Bishop, over the Western Front.

Engine — 260 hp Mercedes
Wingspan — 41 ft. 6 ins.
                          Length — 26 ft. 11 ins.
Weight — 3439 lbs.
Speed — 101 mph at 10,000 ft.
Ceiling — 17,500 ft.
Endurance — 4 hrs.
Armament —1 fixed synchronized Spandau machine gun, 1 flexible Parabellum machine gun in rear

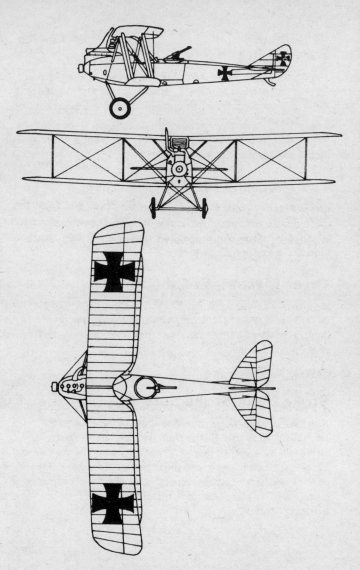

Fig. 15. Rumpler C-V, three-view diagram

Ralph Barker
Survival in the Sky 60p

The doomed flight of the *Bermuda Sky Queen* . . . The Vulcan
bomber that crashed at London Airport . . . Crisis on the Berlin
Airlift . . . The man who fell through the floor of a Boston bomber
and survived!

Fifteen dramas of the air, in peace and war . . . where death is
inches away and all that counts is survival . . .

The Thousand Plan 75p

This is the story of the night of 30/31st May 1942, the story
of the first 1000 bomber raid . . . the brilliant scheme to drop 1400
tons of bombs on Cologne in 90 minutes . . . to destroy a major
industrial target in a single blow . . .

Great Mysteries of the Air 75p

Was Amelia Earhart a prisoner of the Japanese? How did the Duke
of Kent come to die on a Scottish hillside? Why no court of
enquiry for Glenn Miller? Was the Luftwaffe's target Leslie Howard
or Winston Churchill?

'A subject of compelling power' THE AEROPLANE

Strike Hard, Strike Sure 60p

'The desperate attacks on the Maestricht bridges during the
German advance in 1940, the Dam Busters, the daring daylight
attacks on the diesel engine factory at Augsburg and the submarine
building yards at Bremen, and the successful breaching of the walls
of Amiens prison to release Resistance workers under sentence of
death . . .Full of acts of heroism, realism and vitality'
SUNDAY TIMES

Sydney Smith
'Wings' Day 75p

The story of Wing-Commander H.M.A. Day, prisoner extraordinary.

'Wings' Day planned the first escapers' tunnel ; developed elaborate code networks with Britain ; pinned down thousands of German troops to security duties ; and was the only POW to be awarded the DSO for services during captivity.

'He succeeded magnificently in the task set every British POW – to be a thorough nuisance to the Germans' SUNDAY EXPRESS

H. R. Trevor-Roper
The Last Days of Hitler 75p

'An incomparable book, by far the best written on any aspect of the second German war : a book sound in its scholarship, brilliant in its presentation, a delight for historians and laymen alike' A. J. P. TAYLOR

'Absolutely enthralling . . . It is all there, the fantastic comings and goings, Hitler's last-minute marriage to Eva Braun and the supposed suicide and ritual burning of the corpse' DAILY WORKER

Henry Pelling
Winston Churchill £1.95

'Churchill complete, warts and all, cradle to grave, triumphs and disasters . . . as comprehensive a biography as one could wish to read' NEW STATESMAN

'Dr Pelling tells the public, and the private, story with immense skill' GUARDIAN

Quentin Reynolds
They Fought for the Sky 75p

During the fiercer periods of World War I the average life of a pilot was three weeks.

A race apart, these gallant young men of many nations fought a very personal war with true chivalry.

Here is the breathtaking story of the age of flying aces, of famous aircraft and the men who flew them.

Paul Richey
Fighter Pilot 60p

This personal record of the campaign in France from September 1939 to June 1940 was compiled from a series of daily diary notes by a then anonymous Pilot Officer who flew throughout that period with the famous No. I Squadron of the RAF.

'He has written what I believe to be one of the best books to come out of the war . . . There is revealed, for the first time in this war, the mind and general make-up of an RAF pilot, and the beauty of it is that it is told so simply and so humbly . . .' DAILY MAIL

Guy Gibson
Enemy Coast Ahead 80p

'A book more truly racy, or fuller of vitality, gaiety, high spirits and native good sense, is not likely to be written of the RAF . . . Here is the very accent and idiom of Bomber Command, and an emotional picture as complete as we are likely to get of the way its aircrews contrived to do their duty'
TIMES LITERARY SUPPLEMENT

'Everyone should read this unforgettable book' PUNCH

B. H. Liddell Hart
History of the First World War £1.50

'Immensely readable and informative . . . belongs in the possession of anyone interested in what the greatest British military thinker of the century has to say' THE SOLDIER

'It was always his special talent to be able to express military situations in telling and limpid phrases which would stick in the reader's mind' DAILY TELEGRAPH

'Remarkable for its clarity and objectivity, and for analysis undistorted by professional prejudice or by bitterness over the unrecallable past. It remains outstanding : for those familiar with its subject, illuminating and thought-provoking ; for those new to it and wishing to know what happened in World War I, the best place to begin' WESTERN MAIL

History of the Second World War £1.95

Liddell Hart brought his brilliant and original mind to this magnificent narrative of the war — a task which occupied him for over twenty years. Trenchant, searching, thought-provoking, it is military history written with realism and learning, and illuminated with flashes of insight.

'The book has the mark of the author's genius — a lucidity and insight such as no other military writer can match . . . it will long be read with profit and enjoyment by all interested in the military art' ARMY QUARTERLY

Brian Moynahan
Airport International 80p

The sensational book that takes the lid off the world of international air travel. How smugglers operate, and how they're caught . . . when and how luggage is pilfered . . . how air traffic control really works . . . how airports cope with a crash landing . . . which are the dangerous airports that pilots try to avoid . . . your chances of survival in an air crash.

Based on extensive research by Brian Moynahan of the *Sunday Times Insight* team.

Paul Brickhill
The Dambusters 80p

The inspiring story of the RAF's most famous bomber squadron.

17 May 1943 — Over 300 million tons of water crashed into the valleys of the Ruhr — the most audacious bombing attack of the war had breached the giant Moehne and Eder dams.

617 Squadron was specially created for this great raid, using a new secret weapon which had to remain an enigma for many years. In this book its nature is revealed . . .

B. H. Liddell Hart
The Other Side of the Hill £1.25

The classic account of Germany's generals, their rise and fall . . . Here is the Second World War as it was seen by the men who commanded the Panzer Divisions and the might of the Wermacht — a unique account in the annals of human conflict.

'The most formidable military writer of the age' A. J. P. TAYLOR

'Fascinating and even sensational' ROBERT HENRIQUES

Pan Fiction

J. D. Gilman and John Clive
KG 200 95p

They flew Flying Fortresses. They wore American uniforms . . .
but they were Germans! KG 200 — the phantom arm of
Hitler's Luftwaffe. From a secret base in occupied Norway these
crack pilots plan their ultimate mission, the raid that would bring
Allied defeat crashing down from the exploding skies . . .

'Shattering' TELEGRAPH

Ted Willis
The Churchill Commando 75p

Highly efficient, fully-equipped, armed and organized . . . an army
of vigilantes strike at the targets the Government cannot — or dare
not — touch : the hordes of football hooligans, big-time porn
pedlers, red renegades of the left, muggers and child-
kidnappers . . . until, in this Britain of tomorrow — or today —
Churchill's picture, the Commando's symbol, comes to appear in
almost every window . . .

'Terrifyingly plausible . . . only too easy to believe' DAILY MAIL

Colin Forbes
Tramp in Armour 75p

The time is that fateful spring of 1940 when the Panzers rolled
across Northern France with nothing to stop them. Stranded
behind the German lines, a solitary Matilda tank and its crew, led
by the resourceful Sergeant Barnes, scheme, smash and
manoeuvre their way towards Dunkirk.

'A caterpillar-tracked cliff-hanger' DAILY TELEGRAPH

Pan Fiction

Alexander Fullerton
Sixty Minutes for St George 75p

The Royal Navy's desperate raid on the German base at Zeebrugge . . . eleven VCs and hundreds killed or wounded in one of the finest feats of arms of the The Great War. Now a lieutenant in the legendary Dover Patrol, Nick Everard, who won his spurs at Jutland, is second in command of the destroyer *Mackerel* when the Navy goes in on the most daring assault of its history . . .

'Fullerton's speciality is the meticulous recreation of hazardous seamanship, the noise of battle and the minutiae of bloodshed' SUNDAY TIMES

Zeno
The Four Sergeants 75p

Sicily 1943: A sabotage operation behind enemy lines, to blow a bridge behind a Panzer Division and smash Axis withdrawal strategy. The men – a hand-picked Airborne platoon – include a section of German Jews . . . soldiers who can never allow themselve to be taken alive . . .

'In the war yarn class, this book rates high . . . tense, authentic' SUNDAY TELEGRAPH

You can buy these and other Pan Books from booksellers and newsagents; or direct from the following address:
Pan Books, Sales Office, Cavaye Place, London SW10 9PG
Send purchase price plus 20p for the first book and 10p for each additional book, to allow for postage and packing
Prices quoted are applicable in the UK

While every effort is made to keep prices low, it is sometimes necessary to increase prices at short notice. Pan Books reserve the right to show on covers and charge new retail prices which may differ from those advertised in the text or elsewhere.